A CA·PELLA

REV·O·LU·TION

\ ˌä-kə-ˈpe-lə\ \ ˌre-və-ˈlü-shən\

By Professor Griff

D1596792

Acapella Revolution

Photo by Stephanie Deakins
at the Grammy Museum
in Los Angeles May 2012

ACAPELLA REVOLUTION
THE REVOLUTION IN ACAPELLA
BY
PROFESSOR GRIFF
(KAVON SHAH)

A'capella Revolution© 2013 Professor Griff

Note: These individual songs were copyrighted at the time they were written and recorded but having to re copyright them again in this body of work.

First Edition- first printing January 2013
All rights reserved copyright@ 2013
By: Kavon Shah Pka Professor Griff

Published by: Heirz to the Shah
P.O.Box 11902
Atlanta, Ga 30355
Attn: Kavon Shah
Email: Professorgriffpe@gmail.com
678-557-2919
ISBN# 0-9771242-6-6

Dr. Wendy D. Douglas
Literary Consultant
Intelligent Consulting and Publishing
Email: icpcle@gmail.com
440- 447-0527

Cover Design:
Marcus "Society" Effinger

Photography:
Tafari "nuzulu" Melisiwe
kmtvsns@gmail.com

Arlisha "Angel" Sims
Stephanie Deakins

Data collection
Shawn Carter

Transcribing and Proof Reading:
Anjanette L. McGhee/Joell

Typesetting, Proof reading and Transcribing
Latasha Hampton/Moffett

Proof reading
Dave Young

TABLE OF CONTENTS

DEDICATION

This is dedicated to those who are dedicated to the restoration of our artistic culture.

To all those that were, to all those that are, and to all those will be truth tellers, info warriors, infomaniaxz and souljahz in the way of truth, I salute you.

To my brother "Anwar" Ronald "Tweet" Griffin

My Family:

Taqiyyah Khaliese Shah, Rasheem Khaliqq, Khalil Amir, Nailah Miasia,Isa Shah

ACKNOWLEDGMENTS

"I am, because we are, therefore I am,"

------Steve Biko

In the spirit of all those divine names of the creator, I want to acknowledge those that have been a part of my being who I am, and who the world has come to know, who the enemy has grown to hate, seek to silence and who the god-self has come to be. Me.

The Hon. Louis Farrakhan, Sister Ava Muhammad, Tynetta Muhammad, Professor James Smalls, Ray Hagins and the African Village, Mwaulimu K. Bomani Barutiand his Queen "Yaa", Queen Afua, Phil Valentine, Booker T. Coleman, Dr. Francis Cress Welsing, Umar Abdullah Johnson, My family at the Healthful Essence Vegetarian Café (Charles, Princess and my brother Quadro), Calvin Benjimen, Calvin Muhammad out of Birmingham, Demetrius from Birmingham, Jahi "Make it happen" Muhammad, Bro Richard Muhammad (ATL) Professor Rah A. Karim-Kinsey, Lliala O Afrika, My family at Black and Nobel in Philly (Tyson Gravity and Hakeem), Darren Muhammad, Leticia Fitts, To AWP Bro Natee, Anthony Browder.my brothers precise Science Ruff and free, Tafari and my brother Kaba.

A special thanxz to:
Marcus "Society" Effinger, Khari Wynn, Carlton "Chuck D" Ridenhour, Luther "Uncle Luke" Campbell, Tracy "Ice T" Marrow, Thomas De Carlo "Ceelo Green" Callaway, Douglas E."Dougie Fresh" Davis, Ronnie Devoe, Shamari Fears Devoe, Wise Intelligent, Precise Science, Black Dot,

Narubi Selah, Ernest Grant. Public Enemy: Chuck D, Flavor Flav, Terminator X, Bro Mike, Pop Diesel, Bro James Bomb, Bro James Norman, Roger Chillous, Andrew Williams "The Drew" DJ Lord, 'E' Eric Ridenhour, Clifton Johnson, Eric "Vietnam" Sadler, Dan Lugo. Walter Leaphart, Lathan Hodge.

Thanxz to Julee L Milham and Kyle.

I could not have accomplished this music journey without instruction and guidance from Earle Holder at Har-Bal. (Har-Bal) was the result of a collaboration between Paavo Jumppanen, an electrical engineer and an expert in speaker design and room acoustics, and Earle Holder, a highly sought mastering engineer in great demand worldwide, who will be releasing a book named "Mastering Audio Exposed!"

Thanxz to the hard work and dedication to this body of work through, I could not have imagined doing this without the following people.

Anjanette L. McGhee/Joell you have talents and gifts bestowed upon you that one could only dream of having. Embrace them they are yours to keep.

Latasha Hampton/Moffett as we slowly discover who we really are, those qualities you have only come as a result of you being exactly who the creator created you to be. I am forever thankful to you for helping me bring this **"Acapella Revolution"** into a readable body of knowledge.

To my best friend of seventeen years and counting, "Jade Williams". Jay Johnson, Ashton Brown, London and Jordan. I want to give thanxz to her mom and dad and her whole family for allowing me to be in the family all of these years. Debra and James Jones, Glennetta and Marcus Griffin, Marcus, Morgan and Macai Griffin

Thanxz to "Angel" Arlisha M. Sims for watching my back when nobody else would or could.

Give thanx to all those that took this musical journey with me on all of the projects. To the **Griffin family** in Roosevelt Long Island, New York, my mother Louise Griffin who bought my first set of turntables. Nikki Griffin My little sister who seen that I had to have a studio to work out of. The support of my sisters Marva, Pam, Sherba, Sheila, and Rose, and to my brothers Buck Babe), Fats (Alphonzo), Jack (Benny), JJ (jonas), tweet (Anwar, Ronald) and Michael. To my Cousins, nephews and nieces who are coming up behind me to embrace this music I hope this book will serve your thoughts well. Carl T Simpson, Meson Williams and Ernie, The Ernsta from the velt) and Fam. Neal Kelley and Richard Bush. Rahsaan Robinson

To " Spanish Rick" who I DeeJayed with in Freeport against TA (Tony Allen) Andre "Panasonic" in Freeport thanks yall. The original LAD (Last Asiatic Disciples), Jason "JXL", Sean "Patrick X", John Michael Brian, Sean "Life", Bwyze, The AGS (Asiatic Ghetto Soldiers), The Bomb Squad, Hank and Keith Boxley, Eric Sadler, Gary G-Whiz, Terminator X, Society, Lord Mecca, The bald head dread "Buda", Anthony "Tone Control" Mills, Sean "Studdah Man" Devore, Noval, Randy Glaude, Vance Vexed, Jahbad and Keisha, Richard "PowerBorn"

Everette, Dres the Beatnik, Sonja Nicole, Kerwin "Sleek" Young, John Penn, Erroll Moore, David "C-Doc" Snyder, Donta Carfagna, Johnny "Juice" Rosado, Black the Barber, Q-Qass, Laverio "LV" Barnes , Danita Delutcha (the twins) Eroll, Fast Eddie Miller, Dave the non White guy, "Divinity" this female bass player is the truth. Trinity McCullough, Seven X Dominga, brother's keepers from Memphis.

Se7enth Degree album by 7th Octave was released Oct 19, 2004 on the Slam Jamz Recordings label. The 7th Octave: Professor Griff, Society, Power Born (vocals); Khari Wynn (guitar); Jahi Nelson (electric bass); Jahleel Eli (drums); DJ Majestic (turntables). Stahrr The fem Emcee,

The God Damage album by the 7th Octave was released September 20, 2011.Those musical influences are too many to mention both musical and non-musical. Society, Khari Wynn, Tammy Stanko, and Omar Phillips.

To my PE fam (PUBLIC ENEMY) As we head towards the Rock and Roll Hall of Fame together I want you know that if I had to do it all over again.... I would, with every one of ya'll. Yes you too "Flav"
(PE): Chuck D, Flavor Flav, Terminator X, Bro Mike, Pop, James Norman, James Allen, Roger Chillous, Malik Farrakhan (Tony King), Greg Clifton Johnson, DJ Lord, T-Bone, Mike Faulkner Brian Hardgroove, Khari Wynn, Lou and Eric "E", Casper and Sammy.

Give thanxz to Khalid el-Hakim: Outside of music, Professor Griff is also very involved in the Black History 101 Mobile Museum. With museum touring season upon us, Griff stated, **"I would really like to take it a lot**

deeper, man, and start talking about some of those black, historical facts, that we don't get a chance to talk about in the classroom and in the lecture hall and over the dinner table in black homes. The only way other races and cultures are going to appreciate it, is if we, black people, bring it to the damn table." Specifically, Griff is hoping to educate this season's visitors on the creation of Rock music, with an emphasis on black women Rock pioneers, as well as teachings on the black role colonial America and education initiatives.

To those who have help me see this life in black and white with a little bit of color Alex Jones, Jordan Maxwell, Texx Mars. Jim Marrs, Michael Tsarion.

Thank you to Dejuan Boyd, Ben Ransom, Synclair Wright, Chuck Chill Out, DJ Red Alert, Tyra Coles and Demetria (Skinny Chick no#1) Clark Sonia (skinny chick no#3) and Toni Fields from Detroit now in LA skinny chick no#1. Omari Barksdale and Tasleem El-Hakim. Brother Marcus 3X at Nubian bookstore and Sis Nia at Medu Bookstore

To all those I have taken the musical walk through life with and didn't mention you can charge it to my head and not my heart.

All truth passes through three stages. First, it is ridiculed. Second, it is violently opposed. Third, it is accepted as being self-evident.
------ Arthur Schopenhauer

ABOUT THE AUTHOR

 Professor Griff is an internationally renowned educator, writer, producer, musician, platinum recording/spoken word artist, lecturer and one of the Co- founding members of the pioneering and revolutionary hip hop group Public Enemy. Author of the popular music business guide: Musick Bizness R.I.P. (Resource Information Publication), Griff stands as a highly acclaimed, seasoned entertainment industry veteran and sought-after resource on all aspects of the music business. An activist within both the conscious and hip hop communities; Griff currently stands as a permanent fixture on the international lecture circuit with his riveting and powerful discourse/book, the Psychological Covert War on Hip Hop. In 2013 while completing his fourth book **"Acapella Revolution"** Professor Griff was inducted into the Rock and Roll Hall of Fame with Public Enemy.

An energetic and passionate educator, Griff skillfully customizes this extensively documented lecture to suit the needs of all audiences. Armed with an exemplary life of service and an impressive twenty-year musical career, Griff captivates audiences with his universal call for social responsibility within both the hip-hop community and larger culture. As perhaps a testament to his firm commitment to raise the level of consciousness of today's entire hip hop generation; Griff effortlessly draws upon his own extensive entertainment industry experience and a vast reservoir of historical scholarship and research to deliver this poignant message. Reared in Long Island, New York and a current resident of Atlanta, Georgia; Griff maintains a coveted role as Minister of Information for Public Enemy and is currently celebrating an unprecedented sixty world tours and 20th Year Anniversary, with the group. A well-rounded music enthusiast, Griff is also a member of the hip hop/metal band 7th Octave, and has created an empowering youth hip hop curriculum entitled Kidhoppaz, designed to fuse education and entertainment into a positive, effective instructional module. Musically, Griff has recorded nine albums with his group Public Enemy, however he has long distinguished himself as a talented and acclaimed solo artist as well. Namely, while signed to Luke Records Griff wrote, produced and recorded three powerful and thought-provoking albums entitled: Pawns in the Game (1990), Kaoz II Wiz-7-Dome (1991) and Disturb N Tha Peace (1992). Also, in 1998, Griff released Blood of the Profit on Lethal Records. With his group Confrontation Camp, Griff recorded the album Objects in the Mirror May be Closer than they Appear (2000) and The Word Became Flesh (2001) with his group 7th Octave he recorded the album The Seventh Degree (2004) and The God Damage in (2011) Griff has appeared in the following films: **"Turntables"** and **"The Chip Factor"**, in addition he spearheaded the production of the informative documentary entitled **"Turn off Channel Zero"**. Griff holds a Bachelor of Science degree in Education, is a licensed personal security defense instructor, and an accomplished martial artist. An avid lecturer, known for his innate ability to impart life-changing ideas, concepts and techniques for the spiritual/personal growth and development of all who attend his lectures, Professor Griff is uniquely equipped to meet the needs of an international wide-ranging audience.

MOST OF MY HERO'S DON'T APPEAR ON NO STAMP

These lyrics were written and recorded for the song "**Most of my hero's don't appear on no stamp**" but were left out of the song and the album. ----2012

Noise from boys, yea at 510,
Rip the tongue from this Beast.....then get it in

From the rip, P-Griff....broke script, embrace the gift
Load clip, shots licked, from the camp to the stamp, yea no shit
Liberate, love.... hate, naw, ...dig this......

RISE UP warrior, scholars, with a clench fist.
PE on the grind, now print this.
Rage engage, from the page of the Mau Mau
Call the Adon; all Devine evils "bow down"

It takes a nation of millions, yea it did hit
Power rose from the "D" and his sidekick
All praises are due, don't forget this
case this pale face trip ......safety off this

Data check, from a vet this is HIP HOP
Demons vexed from the set.... check, from flav'z clock
From the pin, of the mind, of the minista
Those oppose, step and the S 1's will see ya!

Identify, rebel mind, won't die
P Griff nappy nouns, you can't deny
born n bread Roosevelt yea from LI
connect, left n right brain "THIRD EYE"

---- By: K. Shah pka Professor Griff

FORWARD

By: Dr. Wesley Muhammad, September 24, 2012

January 1, 2012 I was driving home from the Peach Drop in Atlanta, Ga. My 12-year old daughter was riding shotgun and in the back were my son, 9, and their cousins, 10 & 13.

All of a sudden these children break out into a rather detailed and animated discussion about the Illuminati and Hip Hop music. Frankly, I was shocked. I had no idea that my children knew who the Illuminati were much less could discourse (in their pre-teen manner) about them and their 'agents' within Hip Hop. But such was the case. They knew that the Illuminati were a group of old Satanists trying (successfully) to rule the world; they knew that aspects of Hip Hop music and some of its artists have been conscripted into the service of the Illuminati. Oh, and they knew that there were hand signs. The experience for me as I was driving and listening was a bit surreal. What did this tell me? It told me that my Brother Professor Griff has been teaching my children.

And he is teaching countless children across this country, as well as adults like me. This is, in my mind, the greatest achievement of a man whose life is a story of hard-earned success and achievement. I have been to Professor Griff's lectures and seminars on numerous occasions and have left intellectually elevated every time. But his success in shaping and elevating the thinking and discourse of countless young people has to be his greatest contribution to the struggle of his/our community so far. To have young people in 2012 - a notoriously uninformed and uninterested lot - broadly aware of the nefarious clandestine agenda of this world's Secret Government is a phenomenal accomplishment in and of itself; to have them excitedly discoursing about it is, to a great extent, Griff's signature success today. I can confirm that he truly is 'Teaching the Babies'.

Music and entertainment has globally been the social drum-major for quite a while, and in the Black community there has been no social force more influential than Hip Hop in shaping the thinking and culture of this current generation and the one prior. The guardians of White Supremacy know this well and have clearly determined to use Hip Hop to shape Black culture in a way that serves their ends. The effeminization of the Black male in America and the general Nigga-fication of the culture are just two culturally damaging social trends that serve the interests of White Supremacy and which our music (Hip Hop and R&B) have contributed greatly to. Exposing the sinister interests that the guardians of White Supremacy have taken in this profoundly potent social force (Hip Hop) is a true service Professor Griff is providing, not just to the music community and its fans but to the Black community in general. I applaud his effort and am honored to serve with him.

I pledge resistance, To remain in existence
Non violence is what we use, But silence is no excuse
Cultural destruction is achieved by spiritual corruption
Genocide, suicide, homicide deeds
sexism, racism fascism greed.

"Know Applause" this is for the cause

----Professor Griff

HOW TO USE THIS BOOK

Purpose for this book and how to read it:

There are few books that need instructions on how to approach its contents The A'capella Revolution is a body of work that does not require any high degree of artistic merit or reference point to extract its lessons. This book should be read with the concept of "expecting the non-expectation" which simply means, you need to approach it with an expectation of it moving you out of your comfort zone into your collective sub-conscious comfort zone, once you release the "N!&&@ "Freak-Quency" Frequency See *The Meta-pysical Goddesstry of the Soul of Hip Hop"*. You must bring an open mind and a willing spirit of revolutionary change to the mental, intellectual and spiritual meeting point *"The Black Dot"*.

If I were to write a book like this, I think I would start off by saying I would like to write a book that I would like to read and then I would ask myself the question "How do I Read This Book?" This book is about experiencing the thoughts, feelings, emotions and formula that went on in the mindset of one of Hip Hop's "Prophets of Rage" Professor Griff.

This book is a multi-layered construction of a literary work that will consist of multi-dimensions dealing with human life as far as my experiences allowed me to see them. Keep in mind the greatest reality is the un-seen reality. For the person who has become fans of Public Enemy I think this book will serve as a monumental piece, truly a collector's item. When we begin to look into how Public Enemy approached subjects based on conversations, debates and snapping sessions the reader will begin to understand what was needed to take on the task of speaking truth to power, developing the "how to think" instead of being taught "what to think" was very instrumental in how we constructed songs and were able to take those same subjects to the streets and press conferences and ultimately the stage. Myself never taking instructions from outside forces on what to think or the method on how to process thought, I began to construct songs from the conspiratorial point of history. Goodie Mob might have said it best, "The thought process", having the ability to shift your cultural paradigm (your world view) on how to construct a meaningful song that will move people in a real, physical, spiritual and tangible way in this third dimensional paradigm. So the fan will appreciate it on that level, the average reader coming into the knowledge of Professor Griff via Public Enemy or through multi-media or networks, social networks may get a view and a peak into the author and understand the depth of the author via this particular work, "The A'capella Revolution".

On another level the songwriter may appreciate this work simply because the creative writing that went into not only writing the book but writing the songs that make up the book. The songs are written in a very creative writing kind of way not adhering to any standardized kind of way of writing songs. Everything from its use of Ebonics and dealing with different phonetics, dealing with techniques, like the haiku.

Plural haiku Definition of HAIKU
: an unrhymed verse form of Japanese origin having three lines containing usually five, seven, and five syllables respectively; also : a poem in this form usually having a

seasonal reference Haiku are poems written in three short lines. Sometimes they are written in a single line. They can capture a feeling, image or even something less serious. There are two types of haiku: English and Japanese. While they are very similar, you will need to learn more in order to write the perfect haiku.

History and Structure of Haiku Poems

A haiku poem consists of three lines, with the first and last line having 5 moras, and the middle line having 7. A mora is a sound unit, much like a syllable, but is not identical to it. Since the moras do not translate well into English, it has been adapted and syllables are used as moras.

Haiku started out as a popular activity called "tanka" during the 9th to 12th centuries in Japan. It was a progressive poem, where one person would write the first three lines with a 5-7-5 structure, and the next person would add to it a section with a 7-7 structure.

The chain would continue in this fashion. So if you wanted some old examples of haiku poems, you could read the first verse of a "tanka" from the 9th century. The first verse was called a "hokku" and set the mood for the rest of the verses. Sometimes there were hundreds of verses and authors of the "hokku" were often admired for their skill. In the 19th century, the "hokku" took on a life of its own and began to be written and read as an individual poem. The word "haiku" is derived from "hokku." The three masters of "hokku" from the 17th century were Basho, Issa, and Buson. Their work is still the model for haiku writing today. They were poets who wandered the countryside, experiencing life and observing nature, and spent years perfecting their craft.

Haiku Poems From the Masters

A review of haiku poems is an excellent way to become familiar with this form of poetry. Remember that in translation, the moras won't be the same as syllables. In Japanese, there are 5 moras in the first and third line, and 7 in the second, following the 5-7-5 structure of haiku.

Haiku poems date from 9th century Japan to the present day. Haiku is more than a type of poem; it is a way of looking at the physical world and seeing something deeper, like the very nature of existence.

The technique which was developed by the Japanese in which black people in America who understand hip hop and its five elements do naturally. The artist and the poet may dive into some of the storytelling in the book. The artist and the poet may love the format and the arrangement of the songs. So there is something in it for the artist and the poet. Having to perform these songs, coming from the thought to the actual application of writing the song and then bringing the song to life be it via video or on stage in a live show is a beautiful thing for the artist to see coming from concept to completion.

Another level is the researcher and dealing with history. The researcher may look at it like wow. These songs are layered with rhymes and clever lyrics but also jam packed with information that would send the researcher researching. Catchy phrases tend to catch our ear and our imagination but once that fades out what are

you truly left with? This is where myself and Chuck D, as song writers, tend to take the average listener and the seasoned writer/artist.

When a song is constructed it is constructed based on research that was done by the songwriter. It is rare in my case that a song is ever written just off the top of the dome (head) so to speak, if I can use that terminology. So in researching the material that would lay the basis for the song it gives the song depth, to the point where you can speak outside of the context of the 3 and a half minute song the time allowed to the artist by radio air play standards. Thanks to *Gamble and Huff, Smokey Robinson Asford and Simpson, Babyface* and other writers, producers and artists the time it took for what you wanted to express was not an issue. So there the researcher will find joy in knowing that different avenues were taken to construct these particular songs. So the researcher may look at it like it was a wealth of knowledge that was there that laid the basis for the 3 and a half minute song that you may see or hear or read about but mainly hear on an album. Another layer is resources. The book is layered with resources. There is over five different pages of resources that the author used to construct not only the songs but this particular book. Everything from your ***live-it versus your diet.***

There is a list of books and DVD's. There is a list of resources dealing with the New World Order, The Illuminati, Afro-Centered and Afro-Centric education, music and theory, etc. These books, I think are the resources that the reader is looking for in these pages are valuable resources. These examples are to show the reader just what was used to construct songs and develop critical thinking. Those that have heard the songs and seen the live shows, heard the interviews, know that deep research and critical thinking went into the making of what we know today as Public Enemy's "Mind Revolution".

This book may benefit you because it delves into how you balance the spiritual versus the religious in cultural context. There is a song there that speaks to that and that formula is here in the book also. So this is how to read this book written from someone that has approached this particular work as an author-reader, reader-author. As I said in the beginning I want to write a book that I would want to read and that book is "The A'capella Revolution." Here is my formula, use it to your heart's content, but remember......

"Respect the Architect"

---Professor Griff

INTRODUCTION

The A'capella Revolution is......... the Revolution in A'capella.

"The Alchemical Transformation of reconstructing the Oral Tradition "

Quote from the movie Rize...

Definition of: **A CAPPELLA**
a cap·pel·la adverb or adjective \ˌä-kə-ˈpe-lə\
: without instrumental accompaniment

Definition of: Rev·o·lu·tion
rev·o·lu·tion noun \ˌre-və-ˈlü-shən\
a sudden, radical, or complete change

b : a fundamental change in political organization; *especially* : the overthrow or renunciation of one government or ruler and the substitution of another by the governed

c : activity or movement designed to effect fundamental changes in the socioeconomic situation

A'capella being associated with the "oral tradition" and the "Devine Utterances" refers to the transmission of culture *(way of life)* life lessons through vocal utterance, vibration and frequencies. These long held cultural imprints were viewed as master keys. The "oral lore" is cultural material and tradition transmitted orally from one generation to another. The messages or testimony *(Divine instruction)* are verbally transmitted in speech or song and may take the form of a new genre' Hip Hop. The "Opposition to instruments in worship" *(Drum)*, was introduced during slavery and present-day religious bodies known for conducting their worship services without musical accompaniment are often off-shoots of the three major religions. It is the ram horn that calls the "Jews" to prayer, it is the Bell that calls "Christians" to worship and it is the human voice in "Islam" that calls the doers of the will of Allah to receive the guidance to carryout that will. It is the African who has always incorporated the natural vibration of the universe (the Ohm) and the human voice at the "God" Octave that is responsible for calling back together the natural order of things, starting with the "self". The African tradition is responsible for all three major religions to who and what they are.

The science of socializing the thoughts of the listener is the revolutionary method that the A'capella Revolutionary movement will bring about. This "Social Science" is the oratorical discipline that is in practice today to effect society and human behavior. The Creator simply said "Be"....and it is.

The "A ca·pella Rev·o·lu·tion---(\ˌä-kə-ˈpe-lə\ \ˌre-və-ˈlü-shən\) also speaks to the writers ability to understand the oral tradition as it exists in countless numbers of African cultures. We have uncovered that this form of storytelling, spoken word has its roots in a very old but existing art form. The idea of all things we write begin with the thought, and as we are taught the brain was made to think rightly.

These concepts may lay dormant until such time when we need them to carry out that particular idea. These lessons from the past serve as part of the process of bringing about a mind revolution. Through thought we think, then we write, then we vocalize the thought, we may even express the thought through visuals (ie) video's or graf-writing or dancing or a high form of alchemy deejaying. The thoughts become us and we them, as we bring about a revolution of the mind.....in A'capella "The Revolution in A'cappella".

This book explores the formula of those artists that dared to speak truth to power. The formula given to us by "KRS-ONE" entitled "Edu-tainment" the concept of teaching through music, through sound, through the elements *(four elements of Hip Hop)* and synthesized by the 5th element "knowledge of self".

If the hunt is always told by the hunter how will the lion fair?

Our story needs to be told to us by us.

COLOR CONFRONTATION
(Racism White Supremacy)

Color Confrontation, Was recorded in Liberty City, Florida back in 1992, when I was on Luke Skywalker Records after being ousted from Public Enemy. At the time the song was recorded I was studying and doing research on racism white supremacy through the work of Dr. Francis Cress Welsing and Neely Fuller Jr. I based my song on their lifelong body of work. I managed to construct a song from some of the basic lessons learned from that research. Little did I know that this would correspond with the life giving teachings of the most Honorable Elijah Muhammad.

"(The Cress) Color-Confrontation theory postulates that whites desired and still do desire sexual alliances with non-whites, both male and female, because it is only through this route that whites can achieve the illusion of being able to produce color…The extreme rage vented against even the idea of a sexual alliance between the Black male and the white female, which has long been a dominant theme in the white supremacy culture. This is viewed by the Color-Confrontation theory as a result of the white male's intense fear of the Black male's capacity to fulfill the greatest longing of the white female — that of conceiving and birthing a product of color."

Basically back when Chuck D decided to incorporate Dr. Francis Cress Welsing's work,'The Color Confrontation' and the 'Isis Papers', into this quote unquote Public Enemy's outreach work that we were doing in the prisons, in the streets, in the hood, in the drug traps and in the youth centers. It was a very exciting time simply because that body of work I had studied but didn't understand it until I actually went out and seen these things happening as Dr. Francis Cress Welsing laid out in her book. But you kind of figure that if we were dealing with the Cress theory then it was a theory then it needed practical examples with practical applications. So at that particular time there was a lot of racial tension going on. I am only giving you this to give you the backdrop on how I came up with writing the song The Color Confrontation a lot later on. The songs I was writing at that particular time they never needed depth or subject matter. My main problem was, my main struggle was to not make the songs so deep. So if you read Dr. Francis Cress Welsing's work you would have a hard time trying to translate what you know into a sixteen bar verse cause she deals with signs and symbols, symbol formations, thoughts, beats, actions, emotional response so working with a brother named Tone Control, of course Society and Chuck D and other people. These brothers were instrumental in me crafting some of the songs because a lot of times these songs come from conversations we have and they ultimately lead and serve as the basis to songs but I really appreciate Tone Control and Society for creating that spirit around the entire project entitled "Kao's II Wiz-7-Dome". That Kao's II Wiz- 7-Dome Album was very interesting simply because the time in which it is set in. I was out of Public Enemy on Luke's label in Miami having to travel back and forth from Miami to New York. At that particular time I think I was married which was something very deep and interesting in itself. So that Color Confrontation was mainly based on Dr. Francis Cress Welsing's work and just kind of dealing with the racial tension at that particular time. So I managed to construct songs from basic life lessons learned from my research. So let me go into the song and give you examples I used something basic as the colors of the rainbow, which the gay lesbian community took as their flag. But I took those colors to give a certain example on the human family being all races and all colors. So I kind of laid it out and using Dr. Francis Cress Welsing's work I kind of expressed myself and gave examples of a story that I wrote based on the differences and colors and experiences that we go through, which are all laced with racism white supremacy. And that in a nutshell is the Color Confrontation.

Color Confrontation
Written by: K. Shah pka Professor Griff

Color Confrontation
Professor Griff
Title: Disturb N Tha Peace
Label: Skywalker Records
Release Date: 12/10/1992

Verse 1
Brother black is on the right track
He lives in a shack with sista mo black
Now sista mo black had a part-time beef
With Mrs. White She tried to keep her peace
Now Mrs. White like 'em tall, dark and handsome
Dipped in a room with gray But he was short son
Circuit trying to date both tan and off white
But understood she only stood for one night
Now Mr. Green he showed up on the scene
With Mrs. White she tried to beat him for his green
Scooped her up in his rust colored truck
Couldn't get boots so he was shit out of luck
Now Mr. White wasn't really aware
Of how much Mrs. White, Yo she really didn't care
All he knew she had a part-time job
Doing some housework and polishing knobs

Verse 2
Now Mr. White had gotten into a fight
Over the hype you of Mrs. White

Mr. White it was all the same
And Mr. Blue too he played the game
Big brother Brown was down to get down
But little Mrs. White couldn't fool around
For Mr. Red she was waiting for him
Met Ms. Pink downtown in the gym
Now Mr. Blue pushed up but he's a cop
Got too close she said she got to stop
Cause sista cream had burnt brother green
Left him drippin at the clinic it was mean
Big money red owned a lot of beds
Pimp some hoes to get ahead
Now Mrs. White was his number one stunt
Got brother black to smoke a fat blunt

"White men have gone all over the planet and impose themselves sexually on all of the black, brown, red and yellow women, what if, the black, brown, red and yellow men all decided to descend on this".

---Dr. Francis Cress Welsing

Now Mrs. White like 'em tall, dark and handsome
Dipped in a room with gray But he was short son
trying to date both tan and off white
But understood she only stood for one night

"The Color Confrontation theory also explains why Black male's testicles were the body parts that white males attacked in most lynchings: the testicles store powerful color-producing genetic material. Likewise, the repeated and consistent focus on the size of Black males' penises by both white males and females is viewed by this theory as a displacement of the fundamental concern with the genetic color-producing capacity residing in the testicles. Since the fact of color-envy must remain repressed, color-desire can never be mentioned or the entire white psychological structure collapses."

Now Mr. Green he showed up on the scene
With Mrs. White she tried to beat him for his green
Scooped her up in his rust colored truck
Couldn't get the boots so he was shit out of luck
Now Mr. White wasn't really aware
Of how much Mrs. White, Yo she really didn't care
All he knew she had a part-time job
Doing some housework and polishing knobs

"They can compensate for their color inadequacy only by placing themselves in socially superior positions."

Now Mr. White had gotten into a fight
Over the hype you of Mrs. White
Mr. White it was all the same
And Mr. Blue too he played the game
Big brother Brown was down to get down
But little Ms. White couldn't fool around
For Mr. Red she was waiting for him
Met Ms. Pink downtown in the gym
Now Mr. Blue pushed up but he's a cop
Got to close she said she got to stop

"The white personality, in the presence of color, can be stabilized only by keeping Blacks and other non-whites in obviously inferior positions. The situation of mass proximity to Blacks is intolerable to whites because Blacks are inherently more than equal. People of color always will have something highly visible that whites never can have or produce — the genetic factor of color. Always, in the presence of color, whites will feel genetically inferior.

Cause sista cream had burnt brother green
Left him drippin at the clinic it was mean
Big money red owned a lot of beds
Pimp some hoes to get ahead
Now Mrs. White was his number one stunt
Got brother black to smoke a fat blunt

As a black behavioral scientist and practicing psychiatrist, my own functional definition of Racism (White Supremacy) is as follows:
"Racism (White Supremacy) is the local and global power system and dynamic, structured and maintained by persons who classify themselves as white, whether consciously or subconsciously determined, which consists of patterns of perception, logic, symbol formation, thought, speech, action and emotional response, as conducted simultaneously in all areas of people activity (economics, education, entertainment, labor, law, politics, religion, sex and war) for the ultimate purpose of white genetic survival and to prevent white genetic annihilation on planet Earth – a planet upon which the vast majority of people are classified as non-white (black, brown, red and yellow) by white skinned people, and all of the nonwhite people are genetically dominant (in terms of skin coloration) compared to the genetic recessive white skin people".

The system of Racism (White Supremacy) utilizes deceit and violence (inclusive of chemical warfare, biological warfare and psychological warfare), indeed Any Means Necessary, to achieve its ultimate goal objective of white genetic survival and to prevent white genetic annihilation on planet Earth.

In the existing system of Racism (White Supremacy) when the term is undefined and poorly understood there is general confusion and chaos on the part of the victims of that system (local, national and global). It then becomes impossible for the victims of racism (White Supremacy) to effectively counter the global system of Racism (White Supremacy).

The African enslavement, imperialism, colonialism, neo-colonialism, fascism, etc., are all dimensions and aspects of Racism (White Supremacy).

Resource information:

The Isis papers by Dr. Francis Cress Welsing. The United-Independent Compensatory Code/system/concept by Neely Fuller Jr.

THE OLE B#TCH U WORRYZ
(The Illuminati)

The Ole-Bitch U Worryz, was a song I wanted to do, to update the information dealing with the Illuminati. I didn't think I'd get anyone to record it with me, but Chuck D and Kyle Jason stepped up to the plate. Later on we formed a group called *Confrontation Camp*. It was recorded for my album *"Blood of the Profit"* on Lethal Records owned by a friend of mine Ron L. Skoler.

The Ole B#tch U Worryz was a lot more intricate simply because when I signed the deal with a company owned by a very good friend of mine Ron Skoler. I met Ron Skoler in the early days of Public Enemy, he was one of the lawyers that helped ink the deal for Public Enemy. He later on became Manager of Public Enemy along with Ed Choplin who worked on Jimi Hendrix's work. Now I often said to myself this thing served as strange bed fellas because they both became close friends of mine and to a degree they became advisors in business matters. Later on I signed the deal with Lethal Records who was owned by Ron who did a deal with Joan Jet of The Black Hearts. Joan Jet and The Black Hearts they did a deal with Mercury Records and my album Blood of The Profits came through that bloodline so to speak. I know what you are saying strange bed fellas but anyway. As I strengthened my relationship with Steve Cokely and the black community and doing business with black people in the black community and the konscious people community. It never married, I never married it with my business relationship with Ron Skoler and Ed Chaplin in New York. The Ole B#tch U Worryz the song was a song based on the work that I was doing with Steve Cokely and Khalid

Muhammad. I wanted to express to the black community that there is a cobble that's out there – a group of men meeting in secret to determine black people's destiny and as opposed to saying it was the Illuminati, although I did say it in the song, I was spelling out the framework of the Illuminati agenda way back then. I had studied material under Steve Cokely and Khalid Muhammad. As I did the work with Brother Marcus 3X, Corey Johnson and brother Wade in Atlanta. I was well aware of who the Illuminati was and wrote about it in a song way back then so as I began to write over the years Elvis Killed Kennedy was a song in reference to the Illuminati and the New World Order and even the song I did with Black Dot called Right On I spoke about the Illuminati and even recently on a song that I wrote dealing with one of the gentlemen that was overseas which I will mention his name in the book a little bit later on, it was a song entitled Riots of Rage that I did with Chuck D and my son Rasheem Khaliq, that I actually put on my album The God Damage. So that is it in a nutshell about the Ole B#tch U Worryz dealing with the Illuminati.

THE OLE B#TCH U WORRYZ
Written by: K. Shah pka Professor Griff

The Ole B#tch U Worryz
Professor Griff
Title: Blood Of The Profit
Label: Lethal Records
Release Date: 8/18/1998

Verse 1
Behold that pale trick with that tre six
The beast sparks the mark in the dark with some foul shit
Proof of the conspiracy, Seriously see
I ain't got no implantable bio computer chip Flip,
Between reality and uuuuhm insanity
Planted inside of me, I be that PG
Anti-fertility vaccine, Scheme some things,
Death you bring, Fat beats we bring
Verbal venereal treason the reason
King James got the new age tracks
So who you pleasing
P2 lodge shit, let's see you dodge this
Nigga's swishing vote scam douching.

Chorus
(Ole ass bitch dam you, you betta worry
Duck dam the field naggers coming at cha)

Verse 2
Ritz crackers in blue suits

Committed 300 and uhhhhm roundtable groups
Check it
Oppenhimier diamond minings in order
Lead your melaninated daughters to the slaughter

(Chuck D)..........

Professor Griff.........
Regurgitate and refrain from the MK Ultra
Knights of Malta verbal assaults
A culture assault
Caught in a semi counter clockwise revolts no joke

(Chuck D).........

Professor Griff.........
Tragedy and hope nope, You want fax and facts
Then free Geronimo Pratt, With snares and high hats
With black greek boules back packs, Dump that 40 ounce
black

(Chuck D)........

Professor Griff.......
Three degrees of blue deception
Prepare for the reception of this old girls perception
Of this new world order collection of bodies
Brought to you by the Illuminati.

It's not about the east or the west coast, it's not where you're from its where you at yo!, think you gone clown laying s#%! to sound, don't be afraid step up or duck down.

---Kyle "Ice" Jason Smith

Behold that pale trick with that tre six
The beast sparks the mark in the dark with some foul shit

And I looked, and behold a pale horse: and his name that sat on him was Death, and Hell followed with him. And power was given unto them over the fourth part of the earth, to kill with sword, and with hunger, and with death, and with the beasts of the earth.

----- King James Bible

William Cooper, author of "Behold a Pale Horse", The best-selling conspiracy book of all-time, was murdered by agents of the federal government in November 2001, mere weeks after 9/11.

In the words of Bill Cooper himself:
"I have already revealed that I saw that AIDS was man made to eliminate the undesirable elements of society while I was attached to Naval Security and Intelligence."

"...History is replete with whispers of secret societies...
The oldest is the Brotherhood of the Snake, also called the Brotherhood of the Dragon, and it still exists under many different names. The Brotherhood of the Snake is devoted to guarding the 'secrets of the ages' and the recognition of Lucifer as the one and only true God... It's secret symbol is the all-seeing eye in the pyramid."

"...the heart of the Bilderberg Group consists of 39 total members of the Illuminati. The three committees are made up exclusively of members of all different secret groups that make up the Illuminati, the FREEMASONS, the VATICAN, and the BLACK NOBILITY. This committee works year round in offices in Switzerland."

"Cooper states that he has traced the history of the nefarious Illuminati all the way back to the Ancient Temple of Wisdom in Cairo, long before the birth of Christ. 'The Illuminati exist today under many different names and many different occupations.' Cooper told us. 'They practice Hegalian conflict/resolution.' They appear to oppose each other at the bottom ranks, but at the highest levels they are actually organizing and controlling the conflict which they have created to produce the solution that they seek."

"'The Illuminati are extremely powerful, very wealthy men. They believe that they are the guardians of the secrets of the ages. They believe that the vast majority of people would not know what to do with the real knowledge and the real truth and the real science -- and would, in fact, misuse them all. They further believe that everything that they do is for the ultimate betterment and survival of humankind -- even if it means killing two billion people to reach their goal...'"

"We have been taught lies. Reality is not at all what we perceive it to be. We cannot survive any longer by hanging onto the falsehoods of the past."

---William Cooper

Proof of the conspiracy, Seriously see John Robison (1739-1805) was a Scottish scientist, who late in life wrote one of the definitive studies of the Bavarian Illuminati. He was a contemporary and collaborator with James Watt, with whom he worked on an early steam car, contributor to the 1797 Encyclopedia Britannica, professor of philosophy at the University of Edinburgh, and inventor of the siren.

Although Robison was very much an advocate of science and rationalism, in later life, disillusioned by the French Revolution, he became an ardent monarchist. In this work, Proofs of a Conspiracy, Robison laid the groundwork for modern conspiracy theorists by implicating the Bavarian Illuminati as responsible for the excesses of the French Revolution. The Bavarian Illuminati, a rationalist secret society, was founded by Adam Weishaupt in 1776 in what is today Germany. They had an inner core of true believers, who secretly held radical atheist, anti-monarchist and possibly proto-feminist views, at that time considered beyond the pale. They recruited by infiltrating the numerous (and otherwise benign) Freemasonic groups which were active at the time on the continent. Necessarily they had a clandestine, compartmentalized, hierarchical organizational form, which has led some modern conspiracy theorists to identify them as the original Marxist-Leninist group. However, this is most likely simply a case of parallel evolution.

Since we don't have convenient access to the source documents of the Bavarian Illuminati we have to rely on Robison and the Abbé Barruel's Memoirs, Illustrating the History of Jacobinism, both in the 'opposing views' category, for information on this group. The Illuminati have today become a byword for a secret society which hoodwinks its junior members and puppet-masters society at large. This reputation is in no little part due to Robison's book. However, reading between the lines, it becomes obvious that the Bavarian Illuminati were what the American Old Left called a 'talk shop,' barely able to organize a picnic, let alone the Terror. Instead, it seems, they were only expressing views widespread in intellectual circles of the day. They were not, as Robison claims, the fuse that lit the downfall of the French Monarchy. Nonetheless, this book makes fascinating reading, and in conjunction with other historical accounts of the French Revolution, helps dimensionalize the period for students of history.

I ain't got no implantable bio computer chip Flip,
between reality and uuuuhm insanity
Planted inside of me, I be that PG

Revelation 13:16-18: He (The AntiChrist) forced everyone, both small and great, rich and poor, free and slave, to receive a mark in their right hand, or in their foreheads: And no man can buy or sell, unless he had the mark, or the name of the beast, or the number of his name. Here is wisdom. Let him who has understanding count (calculate) the number of the beast: for it is the number of a man; and his number is 666.

Revelation 13:4: And they worshipped the beast (the AntiChrist), saying, "Who is like unto the beast? Who is able to make war with him?"

From an Oct. 11, 1993 "The Washington Times" article entitled, "High-tech national tattoo", by Martin Anderson:

"...There is an identification system made by the Hughes Aircraft Company that you can't lose. It's the syringe implantable transponder. According to promotional literature it is an "ingenious, safe, inexpensive, foolproof and permanent method of

... Identification using radio waves. A tiny microchip, the size of a grain of rice, is simply placed under the skin. It is so designed as to be injected simultaneously with a vaccination or alone."

How does it work? Well, the "chip contains a 10 character alphanumeric identification code that is never duplicated. When a scanner is passed over the chip, the scanner emits a 'beep' and your ... number flashes in the scanner's digital display."

True, an implanted transponder can't yet hold anywhere near as much material as a smart card. But if the desire is there, larger size implants and tiny microchips could soon increase its storage capacity.

Of course, most Americans will find a surgically implanted government microchip repugnant. At least for the foreseeable future, the use of this ingenious device will be confined to its current use: the tracking of dogs, cats, horses and cattle.

But there is no difference in principle between forced to carry a microchip in a plastic card in your wallet or in a little pellet in your arm. The principle that Big Brother has the right to track you is inherent in both. The only difference is a layer of skin.

From the Sat., Oct. 15, 1994 Dr. Fox "ANIMAL DOCTOR" column in the "St. Louis [Missouri] Post-Dispatch":

Dear Dr. Fox: Our local Humane Society has offered, for $25, a lifetime computer chip to be injected with a needle between the shoulder blades of a cat or dog. Apparently, all new animals adopted get a chip. ....

[Dr. Fox:] ...the microchip identification system you describe is an excellent advance in helping with pet loss, owner identification and pet theft.

Microchip ID technology is safe...and adverse reactions following subcutaneous implantation are extremely rare...

From the "Electronic Leash: The Implantable Bio-Chip Is Already Here. Is Big Brother Just Around The Corner?" article by Lisa Crosby in the Vol. 11, No. 14, June 15-June 21 issue of the "Tucson [AZ] Weekly":

.... The size of an uncooked grain of rice, the silicon computer chip...When inserted underneath the skin, this chip can link an individual to a computer database, or it can track a person's location via satellite.

.... Sound impossible? Hardly. Microchip implants are in use as you read this.

....Today, injecting a microchip into animals is routine.....

....Microchip pet identification — technically known as radio frequency identification (RFID) — is available to pet owners nationwide.....

....The concept seems simple. A microchip encased in biomedical-grade glass and imprinted with a unique, unalterable alpha-numeric code. Over 34 billion individual code numbers are available.

....Once implanted, the chip is virtually impossible to remove.... even surgical removal using advanced radiograph techniques is extremely difficult. This is because fibrous tissue adheres to grooves in the glass surrounding the chip to prevent migration of the chip.

...Since the chip operates with low-frequency radio waves and does not contain a battery, it remains passive with no parts to wear out.

Revelation 14:9-11: If any person worships the beast and his image, and receives his mark in their forehead, or in their hand... they shall be tormented with fire and brimstone... And the smoke of their torment will ascend up forever and ever: and they will have no rest day or night, those who worship the beast and his image, and whoever receives the mark of his name.

Matthew 5:30: If your right hand offends you (if it could cause you to sin & miss Heaven), cut it off, and cast it from you: for it is better for you that one of your members (part of your body) should perish, than for your whole body to be cast into hell.

Anti-fertility vaccine, Scheme some things,

Death you bring, Fat beats we bring

Vaccine Dangers
By Ken Adachi <Editor@educate-yourself.org>
http://educate-yourself.org/vcd/index.shtml

The dangers of vaccinations to your child's long term health prospects and longevity itself far outweigh any potential benefits touted by the pharmaceutical industry for vaccines. The LIES and misinformation about vaccine benefits from the drug industry is voluminous, overwhelming, and statistically provable. Don't allow your child to go on the chopping block for these Liars and their profit margins. They aren't working for you, they're servants of the corporate elite/Illuminati and the Illuminati has a surreptitious population reduction agenda in place. Just say NO!

Tell the doctor, tell the clinic, tell the school, tell the nurse, tell the employer, tell the government bureaucrats, tell the health department, or anybody else who is trying to force you or your kids to take vaccines against your will...."Because you must take them", Tell them... NO.

No matter WHAT they say or threaten you with, tell them ....NO.

No vaccines.... ever. Period. You can read why below:

" California Bill 2109 Will Require MANDATORY School Vaccinations Without Signed PERMISSION From MD to Exempt; Sacramento Opposition Rally, on April 17, 2012 (April 14, 2012)

ALL the Vaccines Are Contaminated - Every Last One of Them (Nov. 29, 2011)

"http://educate-yourself.org/vcd/allvaccinescontaminated29nov11.shtml"

The government is planning on forced vaccinations for Swine Flu this Fall. This is a very serious and grave concern for all Americans and people around the world who will be confronted with this issue. You must NOT take these vaccines if you expect to live a normal life span! The purpose behind these vaccinations is population reduction--genocide! Do not believe government PROPAGANDA and lies!

Injunctions Sought to Stop Forced Swine Flu Vaccination Juggernaut (July 22, 2009)

"http://educate-yourself.org/vcd/forcedvaccinationinjunctionsought22jul09.shtml"

Bird Flu (Swine Flu) Hoax Exposed Parts 1 -12 with Dr. A. True Ott~Video

http://www.kickthemallout.com/article.php/Video-Bird_Flu_Hoax_Exposed

Government Created Bio-Weapons & the Genocidal Vaccines Promoted to "Protect" You ~ Video. In Lies We Trust: The CIA, Hollywood and Bioterrorism (2007) with Dr. Len Horowitz (2.5hrs)

http://www.moviesfoundonline.com/in_lies_we_trust.php

Florida State Study Promotes Gardasil 'Benefits', Despite
32 U.S. Deaths to Date (June 4, 2009)
http://educate-
yourself.org/cn/hpvshotmennotconvicnced03jun09.shtml

Insane NY Bill Makes All Federal Vaccines Mandatory
(May   30,2008)
"http://educateyourself.org/cn/NYmandatoryvaccinebill2
9may08.shtml"

Why You Should Avoid Ever Taking Vaccines (Feb. 15,
2007)http://educate-
yourself.org/vcd/howensteinwhyyoushouldavoidvaccines
03feb07.shtml

Vaccine Dangers
Dispelling Vaccination Myths
http://educate-
yourself.org/vcd/phillipsvaccinationnythsmay01.shtml
Vaccination Liberation. http://www.vaclib.org

A top web site for info on vaccine dangers and what to do
to avoid 'mandatory' vaccination. For more info, contact
Donna   Carillo   or   Ingri   Cassel:
<Services4Health@aol.com >

1. To   obtain   school   vaccine   exemption   forms:
(http://www.vaclib.org/exemption.htm)

2. State by State Anti-vaccine

    Resources:
(http://www.vacilb.org/legal/statesource.htm)

Verbal venereal treason the reason

King James got the new age tracks
So who you pleasing

trea·son a> [tree-zuhn] (noun)
1. the offense of acting to overthrow one's government or to harm or kill its sovereign.
2. a violation of allegiance to one's sovereign or to one's state.
3. the betrayal of a trust or confidence; breach of faith; treachery.

With the death of Queen Elizabeth I, Prince James VI of Scotland became King James I of England. The Protestant clergy approached the new King in 1604 and announced their desire for a new translation to replace the Bishop's Bible first printed in 1568. They knew that the Geneva Version had won the hearts of the people because of its excellent scholarship, accuracy, and exhaustive commentary. However, they did not want the controversial marginal notes (proclaiming the Pope an Anti-Christ, etc.) Essentially, the leaders of the church desired a Bible for the people, with scriptural references only for word clarification or cross-references.

This "translation to end all translations" (for a while at least) was the result of the combined effort of about fifty scholars. They took into consideration: The Tyndale New Testament, The Coverdale Bible, The Matthews Bible, The Great Bible, The Geneva Bible, and even the Rheims New Testament. The great revision of the Bishop's Bible had begun. From 1605 to 1606 the scholars engaged in private research. From 1607 to 1609 the work was assembled. In 1610 the work went to press, and in 1611 the first of the huge (16 inch tall) pulpit folios known today as "The 1611 King James Bible" came off the printing press. A typographical discrepancy in Ruth 3:15 rendered a pronoun "He" instead of "She" in that verse in some printings. This caused some of the 1611 First Editions to be known by collectors as "He" Bibles, and others as "She" Bibles. Starting just one year after the huge 1611 pulpit-size King James Bibles were printed and chained to every church pulpit in England; printing then began on the earliest normal-size printings of the King James Bible. These were produced so individuals could have their own personal copy of the Bible.

The Authorized King James Version of the Bible has been cherished and read by Christians all over the world since 1611 when it was published. Sir Winston Churchill said, "The scholars who produced this masterpiece are mostly unknown and unremembered. But they forged an enduring link, literary and religious, between the English-speaking people of the world."

Thus, it is of great significance that all these Satanic symbols were originally placed on the original 1611 KJV Bible. The Rosicrucians who created these symbols really and truly believed that they were creating "centers of occult power" which would throb with demonic power 24 hours per day, 7 days per week. I believe that Bacon and King James firmly intended to create a Rosicrucian Bible, filled with occult symbols which were "throbbing with Satanic power", designed to move the entire English-speaking people of the world into the "Mystic Christianity" called Rosicrucianism.

And, of course, Pilgrim and Puritan leaders of the day knew this belief, because they were "aware of Satan's devices"; within seconds, these genuine Christian leaders would have recognized these symbols, knew of the importance placed on them by Satanists and were able to quickly reject the original 1611 King James Version of the Bible as a "wicked .... Bible from that wicked King!"

Freemasonry and the Bible...From the first Hebrew texts upon papyrus and leather scrolls, the Old Testament, as we know it, today, comes down to us, through the ages.

Q: Why is a basic understanding of Bible genealogy important to a Freemason, today?
A: The reason is that Freemasonry has biblical foundations.

Q: Is a Freemason Bible any different than a regular Bible?
A: No.

The Bible (from the Greek word, biblia) is for all Christians the most sacred of books, the source of truth and the revelation of God's word. Throughout the millenniums (thousands of years), no other book has been reproduced and translated as many times as the Bible.

No original manuscripts are known to exist...only copies of copies and via the many translations, many errors have invariably crept in. Written some 3300 years ago (1300 B.C.-100 A.D.), the Bible continues to be, by far, the most popular of books.

Much of Freemasonry is based upon biblical scripture and biblical characters.

Foundations of Freemasonry and the Bible

For Christians, Freemasonry and the Bible are intricately connected....just as the Holy Books of other religions are central to their Freemason foundations.

The Creator: It is to the Supreme Architect of the Universe, our Creator, he of many names around the world, that each of us worship.

Masonic Symbols: Ark of the Covenant, the Mosaic Pavement, Jacob's Ladder, the Lambskin Apron, King Solomon's Temple and others.

Masonic Ritual Degree Verses: The 3 verses within the 3 Masonic Degrees of Entered Apprentice, Fellow Craft and Master Mason are direct quotes from the Bible.

Biblical Characters: King Solomon, Hiram Abif, Hiram of Tyre, Tubal Cain, St. John the Baptist, St. John the Evangelist, Jacob and Jacob's Ladder, etc. All are biblical characters.

Masonic Altar: The Masonic altar holds a Holy Book (or several Holy Books, depending upon the personal religions of its members). It is around this Holy book that Freemasons circumambulate in their attempts to perform acts pleasing to the Creator.

Masonic Charity: The origins of Masonic charity begin with The Good Samaritan. (Luke 10:25-37)

And so it is written that no man should ever engage in any important undertaking without first invoking the aid and blessing of Deity.

P2 lodge shit, lets see you dodge this
nigga's swishing vote scam douching.

"God's Banker" Freemason Roberto Calvi, member elite Grand Orient of Italy Lodge 'P2'. After fleeing Italy in 1982 Brother Calvi is found hanging under London's Blackfriars Bridge (one of the symbols used by Italian Freemasonry being a Black Friar), his pockets stuffed with five kilos of bricks and rocks (i.e. masonry), his feet dangling in the ebb and flow of the tide (another Masonic inference from their infamous Secrecy Penalty Blood Oaths). British Police rule the death a suicide.

Ritz crackers in blue suits
Committed 300 and uhhhhm roundtable groups
Check it

Four programs on state television (RAI) allege that the CIA paid Lucio Gelli to "forment terrorist activities. "In the first programme someone described simply as "Agent Zero" described how Palme (Prime Minister of Sweden Olaf Palme) had been caught in a deal between the CIA and Iran to release American hostages in Tehran. "Palme was a fly in the ointment so we got P2 to rub him out," the agent said. The second programme, which showed the gaunt silhouette of "Agent Zero One", alleged that P2 was not wound up in the mid-1980s, after the arrest of its leader Licio Gelli. "It still exists. It calls itself P7," he said. According to the agent, the lodge is still functioning with branches in Austria, Switzerland and East Germany. "Zero

One" has now been revealed by the Italian press to be Dick Brenneke, allegedly a career CIA officer"

Richard Bassett, Times ; September 24, 1990

Oppenheimer diamond minds in order

According to the records of the British East India Company, Jewish traders controlled virtually the entire world diamond traffic by the end of the eighteenth century. The Brazilian fields, however, were becoming rapidly depleted of diamonds, and no more diamonds were coming out of India. Just as it appeared that the world might run out of diamonds, the South African mines were discovered in the eighteen-sixties.

The ten leading Jewish merchants in London, fearing that the market would be flooded with South African diamonds, quickly formed a syndicate to buy up all of the production from these new mines. A number of the merchants in this syndicate had also acquired large stock holdings in the De Beers monopoly itself. One of the merchants who took the lead in arranging the deal with Cecil Rhodes was Dunkelsbuhler. Dunkelsbuhler brought into his London company a sixteen year old apprentice from Friedberg, Germany. He was Ernest Oppenheimer, and he would complete the diamond invention.

Oppenheimer came from a large German Jewish family and had two brothers and three cousins who worked in the diamond syndicate. Thus, even as he began as a Junior clerk in Dunkelsbuhler's London office, Oppenheimer was well connected in the diamond world.

He began by sorting rough diamonds, under the supervision of his brother Louis. Louis Oppenheimer not only managed Dunkelsbuhler in London but also coordinated the pricing and classification of diamonds in all the other firms in the syndicate. During this period, Ernest Oppenheimer read all the correspondence that came in from Dunkelsbuhler's representative in Kimberley. Almost from the beginning, he had his heart set on going to the diamond fields, according to a memoir by a diamond sorter who worked with him. "Ernest had bought a six-penny book, in which he carefully noted, meticulously ordered, everything that might be conceivably of some use to him," the sorter, Etienne Fallek, later recalled.

Finally, in 1902, his brother dispatched Ernest to South Africa to run Dunkelsbuhler's small buying office in Kimberley. His salary was 500 pounds a year. He was in many ways the prototype of the multinational businessman: German by birth, British by naturalization, Jewish by religion, and South African by residence.

He usually wore a white starched collar, a dark tie and a long frock coat. He rarely spoke to his fellow workers and he always kept his notebook at his side. Although some of the other sorters in the office simply assumed that he was a compulsive scribbler, Oppenheimer was in fact preparing a detailed analysis of the diamond-mining business. He had an excellent vantage point. Diamonds poured into the office from all the mines in Africa and were graded according to weight, size, shape, color and quality. By studying the records in the office, he was able to determine both the special characteristics and profitability of the production of each mine.

He also traveled around to the independent diggings around Orange River to buy diamonds and evaluate claims for Dunkelsbuhler. It was all part of his education in the diamond business.

In 1908, his cousin Frederick Hirschhorn became the syndicate's chief representative in Kimberley. Oppenheimer, who was close to his cousin, spent considerable time at the syndicate's sorting room. Here he became familiar with the way in which the diamonds were divided among the members of the syndicate and the particular categories of diamonds that the various syndicate members preferred.

Oppenheimer's initial success in acquiring capital came, however, from gold rather than diamond mines. A group of German investors, who were clients of Dunkelsbuhler, wanted to invest in gold properties in the Transvaal, and Oppenheimer arranged for them to buy an interest in operating gold mines. In making these deals, he took for himself a small percentage of the venture, as well as an option to increase his participation at a future date.

By 1914, the Germans had sunk an enormous amount of capital into expanding these gold mines. The outbreak of the First World War made their investment increasingly precarious: Germany was, after all, now an enemy of the British Commonwealth. Moreover, there were constant demands in the press for the expropriation of enemy assets in South Africa. As the pressure mounted on the South African government, Oppenheimer found a solution for the German investors. He personally created an international corporation in which the German interest could be subtly diffused with those of investors of other nationalities. He blended into this new corporation the percentages and options that he had obtained as a deal maker and also a number of interests that had been acquired by his cousins and other relatives in South Africa.

To avoid drawing any unnecessary attention to the German investments, he proposed giving the corporation a name that would strongly suggest an "American connection," as Oppenheimer put it. In a letter to his associates, he wrote, "Our aim should be for our company to make its debut as a new factor in South African finance." After considering the name United South Africa Company, which would be abbreviated USA Company, and then the Afro-American Company, they finally decided on the Anglo-American Corporation, which sounded very much like the Anglo-American alliance that was then winning the war. The mask seemed to work at least with the South African press: when the new corporation was announced in September 1917, the Rand Daily Mail proclaimed in a headline, "American Millions for the Rand."

After establishing his corporation, Oppenheimer quickly shifted his attention from gold back to diamonds. As early as 1910, he had concluded in a memorandum that "the only way to increase the value of diamonds is to make them scarce, that is, to reduce production." He believed that De Beers could bring about such scarcity but only if it expanded its reach beyond the borders of South Africa. He viewed control of the South African mines as a necessary, but not sufficient, condition for an effective diamond monopoly.

Lead your melaninated daughters to the slaughter

Your Brain & Nerves Cannot

Operate Without Black Melanin!
suzar.com/BOTW/BOTW-ch5a-pages53-54.html

Your brain and body can't function without Black Melanin!

Brain, Neuron few people know that Melanin is found in almost every organ of the body and is necessary in order for the brain and nerves to operate, the eyes to see, and the cells to reproduce!

Thus, Melanin is vastly more than just a "pigment" coloring the skin and hair. At the core of your brain is the "locus coeruleus," a structure that is BLACK because it contains large amounts of Melanin which is essential in order for it to operate!

In fact, all the most crucial brain structures are heavily melanized! "Brain melanin is concentrated in a region that functions as a gate for all sensory, motor, emotional and motivational input and output" as well as a region that mediates conscious awareness in general.

Dr. Richard King considers the presence of Melanin to be a key agent in heightening psychic sensitivity in the human organism. Dr. Frank Barr suggests (neuro) Melanin may join forces with the glial cells (formerly seen as only the 'glue' of the nervous system) to form a subtly triggered matrix for mental organization- that is, the "mind's eye."

Melanin in the Brain increases from the lower primates and reaches its peak in the BLACK HUMAN.

"All humans possess this Black internal brain evidence of their common Black Afrikan Origin. The All Black neuromelanin nerve tract of the brain is profound proof that the human race is a Black race, with many variations of Black, from Black-Black to White-Black, all internally rooted in a vast sea of Brain Blackness."

"Humanity may differ in outer appearance, with variations of colors but internally they are all black, all African at the core. The question for all humans is how to relate to this blackness. A transformation process requires, first, the right heart or feelings and profound African knowledge as taught in ancient African universities. Today's racist is afraid, ignorant of his/her blackness, choosing to run from the ancestral Black core. Today's reborn black masters will accept their blackness, become unified with the universe and be inspired to creative genius at levels that surpass the pyramids."

Dr. Richard King
African Origin of Biological Psychiatry (p31, 24)
Nervous System
Page 54

*Melanin is found everywhere, throughout Nature... in animals, plants (that's why raisins and banana bruises are brown), the soil, waters of creeks, lakes, seas, and even in comets! Concentrations vary from parts per million to parts per billion, and it is soluble in liquid phases.

* Melanin is necessary for humans to reproduce!

*Melanin is abundantly present at the inception of life: a Melanin sheath covers both the sperm and the egg! In the human embryo, the melanocytes (skin pigment cells), the brain, and the nerve cells all originate from the same place; the neural crest. Melanocytes resemble nerve cells and are essential for conveying energy. When the presence of Melanin is missing or insufficient in the ectoderm, this causes the mother to lose her baby; in the case of all whites, a defective baby is produced.

*Melanin is the major organizing molecule in living systems.

*Dr. Frank Barr, pioneering discoverer of Melanin's organizing ability and other properties, opens his technical work, Melanin: The Organizing Molecule: "The hypothesis is advanced that (neuro) melanin (in conjunction with other pigment molecules such as the isopentenoids) functions as the major organizational molecule in living systems."

*Melanin is depicted as an organizational "trigger" capable of using established properties such as photon-(electron)- photon conversions, free radical-redox mechanism, ion exchange mechanisms, ion exchange mechanisms, and semi conductive switching capabilities to direct energy to strategic molecular systems and sensitive hierarchies of protein enzyme cascades. Melanin is held capable of regulating a wide range of molecular interactions and metabolic processes."

*Melanin's Main Properties: It absorbs, stores & transforms energy. It has "black hole" properties.

* Black Melanin can convert light energy to sound energy and back again!

* Melanin is BLACK because its chemical structure allows no energy to escape. It is also Black because Black is the perfect absorber of light and all energy frequencies, making Black Melanin the super absorber of Energy and Light! Thus scientists describe it as acting like a "black hole."

* Melanin can rearrange its chemical structure to absorb ALL energy across the radiant energy spectrum (sunlight, X-rays, music, sound, radar, radio waves...) -and can transmute and store this energy for later use!

* Melanin can absorb a great amount of energy and yet not produce a tremendous amount of heat when it absorbs this energy, because it can transform harmful energy into useful energy. According to Dr. Leon Edelstein;

*Melanin can absorb tremendous quantities of energy of all kinds, including energy from sunlight, x-ray machines, and energy that is formed within cells during the metabolism of cells. He theorizes that Melanin has the ability to neutralize the potentially harmful effects of these energies.

* In Dr. Frank Barr's theory, matter is shaped and structured by light: that is, matter is organized through the interaction of molecules composed of slowed-down light. These molecular [Melanin] combinations "eat" light in order to maintain, expand and evolve matter. The more highly evolved a species, the more complex its biological capacity to use light.

* Melanin has superconducting properties; it shows evidence of being a room-temperature (biological) superconductor. Normally, superconductivity occurs only at very low temperatures.

* Melanin is like a battery. Melanin "may be viewed as a battery that is partially charged and can always accept an electrical charge!" When sunlight or other energy comes in contact with the Melanin battery, it increases the charge of the battery to a certain degree. When the energy is captured, the battery has more energy to use in the body. "This means that the BLACK HUMAN can charge up his MELANIN just by being in the sun or around the right type of musical sounds or other energy sources."

* Melanin in the eye receives light and converts it into the electrical energy that comes across as an image.

Regurgitate and refrain from the MK Ultra

Knights of Malta verbal assaults

A culture assault

Caught in a semi counter clockwise revolts no joke

GHETTO INFORMANT PROGRAM & OAKLAND'S BLACK MANCHURIAN CANDIDATES

In 1967, as part of the overall effort of COINTELPRO, the FBI developed a network and list of some 4,000 Black collaborators, assembled from what had previously been codenamed the TOPLEV ("Top Level" Black Community Leadership Program) to inform, disrupt, and aid in obliterating the Black Nationalist and Civil Rights Movement in America. The FBI's BLACPRO ("Black

Program") called the "Ghetto Informant Program" was the list of its over 7,000 new collaborator recruits. [1]

From these networks, I suspect that individuals were carefully selected from the list of new collaborators by other governmental agencies such as the CIA's OPERATION CHAOS which also began in 1967 [2] for top secret classified MK ULTRA projects, then by stealth and deceit mercilessly turned them into guinea pigs. They became experimental subjects of some of the most far reaching technologies of the Twentieth Century such as Tesla technologies.

Former U.S. Air Force Sergeant Sebron Flenaugh, Jr. and his brother Ronnie's timetable to becoming Black Manchurian Candidates also began in 1967 with the inception of "Ghetto Informant Program" and OPERATION CHAOS.

It was the 1950s, a time of doo-wop, sock hops and Bobby Rydell, when Americans dusted off the remnants of WWII and looked toward a more optimistic society. Or so it's often thought. But the '50s were often less Happy Days and more The Day the Earth Stood Still, as fears of a Cold War and mistrust of the government were just beginning to bloom. Since those fears couldn't always be talked about, they came through in films like Invasion of the Body Snatchers, with themes of technology run riot and the loss of free will.

These "delusional fears" were actually rooted in reality, as the government was taking steps toward turning American soldiers into unthinking, unfeeling machines with help from brainwashing and LSD. The CIA, while learning how to bring down Communists, was also learning from them — specifically how they used mind control on Korean War prisoners. Could this mind control also create a zombie-like US soldier, one who would follow orders no matter how grisly, or withstand any amount of torture if captured?

The combination of hypnosis, shock therapy and drugs like LSD and Ketamine made this seem a possibility, and were investigated in a mind control research program called MK-ULTRA. MK-ULTRA was funded by millions of U.S. dollars and led by a scientist named Sidney Gottlieb. In his book The Very Best Men, Evan Thomas describes Gottlieb as "born with a club foot and a stutter, he compensated by becoming an expert folk dancer and obtaining a Ph.D. from Cal Tech ... he drank only goat's milk and grew Christmas trees, which he sold at a roadside stand." That is, when he wasn't drugging research subjects.

The goals of MK-ULTRA included investigating the following:

Materials which will render the induction of hypnosis easier or otherwise enhance its usefulness.

Substances which will enhance the ability of individuals to withstand privation, torture and coercion during interrogation and so-called "brain-washing".

Materials and physical methods which will produce amnesia for events preceding and during their use.

Physical methods of producing shock and confusion over extended periods of time and capable of surreptitious use.

A knockout pill which could surreptitiously be administered in drinks, food, cigarettes, as an aerosol, etc., which will be safe to use, provide a maximum of amnesia, and be suitable for use by agent types on an ad hoc basis.

Tragedy and hope nope, You want fax and facts

The argument that the two parties should represent opposed ideals and policies, one, perhaps, of the Right and the other of the Left, is a foolish idea acceptable only to the doctrinaire and academic thinkers. Instead, the two parties should be almost identical, so that the American people can "throw the rascals out" at any election without leading to any profound or extreme shifts in policy.
Carrol Quigley, Tragedy and Hope

Then free Geronimo Pratt, Which lives in high hats

Born Elmer Gerard Pratt in Louisiana, 1947; died June 2, 2011; son of Eunice Petty Pratt and her husband, a scrap metal dealer; married Sandra Pratt, who was murdered in 1971; married Asahki Ji Jaga, 1976 (the couple divorced in 1995, but later planned to remarry); two children (conceived during conjugal visits), Hiroji and Shona.
Education: University of California at Los Angeles.
Politics: Radical left; former member of the Black Panther Party.
Religion: Catholic.
Memberships: Black Panther Party, 1968-72.

Career: Long-range reconnaissance expert with the 82nd Airborne, 1965-68; Deputy Minister of Defense, Black Panther Party, 1969-72; incarcerated in California for the murder of Caroline Olsen, 1968-97; conviction overturned 1997.

Life's Work: The Black Panther Party, founded in Oakland, California, in 1966, was a radical African American political group that grew out of frustration with the nonviolent approach of the civil rights movement. Known for their uniform of black berets and leather jackets, the Panthers openly armed themselves, engaged in shootouts with police, and basically "scared the hell out of white America," in the words of Mary A. Fischer, as stated in GQ. The Panthers called for violent revolution, and the police took them at their word; then-FBI director J. Edgar Hoover called the group the most dangerous threat to American national security.

With black Greek boules back packs, Dump that 40 ounce black

Sigma Pi Phi Fraternity Incorporated, founded May 15, 1904 in Philadelphia, Pennsylvania. This is the 1st black fraternity in America and was before the 1st black "college" frat, Alpha Phi Alpha Fraternity Incorporated which was founded December 4, 1906. The Boule' is a black GREEK secret society based on another secret society founded at Yale University called Skull & Bones. The Boule's primary founder was Dr. Henry Minton (along with Dr.'s Eugene T. Henson, Edwin Clarence Howard, Algernon Brashear Jackson, Robert Jones Abele and Richard John Warrick) of Philadelphia.

Dr. Henry Minton
The founding member of the New York City chapter, WEB DuBois, said the Boule' was created to:
"Keep the black professional away from the ranks of Marcus Garvey."

(One thing that needs to be pointed out is the time period. Shortly after the founding of the Boule' was also the time Marcus Garvey's "Back to Afrika" movement was reaching a million-plus people without TV or radio.)

DuBois emphasized, as Cokely stated:

"The importance to steal the black professional away from Garvey because an Afrocentric organization that articulated and captured the black professional would give YT no safe haven in the black community, so the Boule' — the remaking of the house negro was necessary to build a group of negroes who had an investment in protecting the white system as produced by YT having stolen this land...This is post reconstruction. Taking away the articulate negro, now desiring to replace them with organized institutions to keep them away from self improvement. So we find in the same period, as the founding of the Boule', the founding of the 4 black male (Alpha Phi Alpha, Kappa Alpha Psi, Omega Psi Phi, and Phi Beta Sigma) and 4 black female (Alpha Kappa Alpha, Delta Sigma Theta, Zeta Phi Beta, and Sigma Gamma Rho) college-based fraternities and sororities...We also find the founding of the NAACP and Urban League."

DuBois was one of the strongest opponents of Garvey and was an instrumental "tool" in stopping one of the strongest grassroots movements in this century. What was Garvey's plan? His plan was to take as many Afrikans from the America's and start a settlement in the nation of Liberia and then help their new nation produce and control their own rubber crops and other industries in natural resources.

Garvey said:

"If the oil of Afrika is good for Rockefeller's interest; if iron is good for Carnegie trust; then these minerals are good for us. Why should we allow Wall Street and the capitalist group of America and other countries exploit our country when they refuse to give us a fair chance in the countries of our adoption? Why should not Afrika give to the world its black Rockefeller, Rothschild, and Henry Ford?"

DuBois, along with Alain Locke — the first black (Cecil) Rhodes Scholar — publicly defiled Garvey by calling him a "gorilla" any chance they got. Locke was quoted as saying:

"We hope the white man deliver's cause we crushed a great black thing, but we know he'll deliver or our people will attack and plague us forever more."

These two house negroes made a bet that YT would come out on top and give a certain percentage of these greedy negroes, namely Boule' members, the wealth they stole from Afrika. What's deep is they didn't believe in Afrikan self-reliance and preferred YT to give them table scraps instead of us making the whole pie!

Understand the Boule' represents the weakest element of Afrikan people. As Cokely puts it:

"It took a type of nigger to form an organization like this. I mean, we just got our asses kicked during reconstruction, Afrika was divided before our very eyes (The Berlin conference), damn, this was 50 years before Rosa Parks!"

The question is why were these black devils like this? The answer may lie in the fact that the Boule' is a GREEK organization.

The name Boule' is a Greek term, meaning "advisor's to the king". The question is, who's the king? The king that they advise, or protect, are the white secret societies responsible for white supremacy: the first white Greek fraternity, Phi Beta Kappa, the Illuminati, Rhodes/Rothschild secret society, Skull & Bones, the Masons, the Round Table Group, The New World Order, One World Government, the Carnegie, Mellon, Rhodes, Milner's Kindergarten, The Rhodes Crown, Times Crown, All Souls Group, Clevedine Sect, and numerous other wealthy family organizations (all are simply alias' and go by many names, but consist of the same members and ideology). These white beasts have raped, murdered & colonized our people for hundreds of years and their children continue the genocide against people of color around the globe.

One of the problems we should have with the Boule' (and the off springs of the Boule', the other 8 college frats and sororities) is that they falsely acknowledge the GREEKS as the founders of civilization. We of course know this is a lie. We know that the Greeks got their knowledge from the Nile Valley (ancient Kemet and Ethiopia — where the original Afrikan man and woman evolved), and they plagiarized (after killing us off and raping KMT, deemed themselves as the originators of the knowledge we gave them) our history and sought to erase the Afrikan presence of KMT. We know that Pythagoras did not create a theorem, but that he stole it from our ancient Afrikan mystery schools.

Who is the Boule'? They are the so-called "talented 10th". DuBois is famous for speaking of (it must also be noted that DuBois' boy, Locke, was a faggot. DuBois was also perceived to have homosexual tendencies). They are a mutation of a white man that seeks to represent something he is not (GREEK). They are "prominent" blacks white America gave to us. Collectively, all 5000+ members and 112 chapters throughout the United States and West Indies making up the wealthiest group of black men on the planet — and to think, none are working in the interest of black people; but, rather, gets a kick out of holding YT's penis as he pisses on people of color. See, the house nigga/field Afrikan theory ain't dead!

Three degrees of blue deception
Prepare for the reception of this old girls perception

The Symbolic (Blue) Lodge, From Quick Index to Masonic information

The Symbolic Lodge (also known as the Ancient Craft Lodge, the St. John's Lodge, and most commonly as the Blue Lodge) is the fundamental body of Freemasonry. No other part of Masonry is accessible until one has received the three degrees of the Symbolic Rite. Admission to membership in the Lodge, as in any body of Masonry, is by petition. Freemasons do not recruit members. (Some jurisdictions have allowed a very limited form of inquiry by a Mason to a friend who might be qualified to become a Mason.) A man who wishes to join the Lodge must request a petition from a Brother. The basic qualifications for membership are that a man be of lawful age (which depends on the jurisdiction; in some states it is 18, and in others, 21), believe in a Supreme Being, be of good character, and request the privilege of membership of his own free choice. There is a fee for the degrees (not unlike tuition for other kinds of instruction), and at least a portion thereof must accompany the petition in most jurisdictions.

Once a petition has been received, the applicant's character will be investigated by a committee appointed for that purpose. After the committee's report is received, the candidate will be balloted on at a meeting of the Lodge. A unanimous ballot is required for election to receive the degrees. (In some jurisdictions, no more than one negative vote.) Not everyone is elected. (It is for this reason that traditionally the applicant must request the privilege of petitioning; in case of rejection, he cannot claim that his friend solicited his membership but was unable to keep his promise.)

The Blue Lodge consists of three separate degrees.
"The word degree, in its primitive meaning, signifies a step. The degrees of Freemasonry are, then, the steps by which the candidate ascends from a lower to a higher condition of knowledge." Albert G. Mackey, The Encyclopedia of Freemasonry, 1873.

The degrees are: Entered Apprentice, FellowCraft, and Master Mason. Each of the degrees requires the candidate to participate in the drama being presented. They are all of a very serious nature and not in the least demeaning of the candidate. Masonic catechisms are a series of memorized questions and answers pertaining to a specific degree. Usually, the candidate meets with a lodge member who knows these catechisms and helps him to memorize the work. The catechisms simply reiterate the degree work that the candidate recently completed and proves his proficiency with them. Once a catechism is completed the candidate can proceed to the next degree.

Of this new world order collection of bodies
Brought to you by the Illuminati.

The word Illuminati means 1. People claiming to be unusually enlightened with regard to a subject. 2. Illuminati Any of various groups claiming special religious enlightenment. Latin ill min t, from pl. of ill min tus, past participle of ill min re, to light up.

The Illuminati are the top players on the International playground, basically belonging to the thirteen of the wealthiest families in the world, and they are the men who really rule the world from behind the scenes (yes, they are mostly men, with a few exceptions). They are the REAL Decision Makers, who make up the rules for presidents and governments to follow, and they are often held from public scrutiny, as their action can't stand scrutiny. They are connected by bloodlines going back thousands and thousands of years in time, and they are very careful keeping those bloodlines as pure as possible from generation to generation. The only way to do so is by interbreeding. That is why you so often see royalties marry royalties, for example. Their parents decide whom their children should marry.

Their power lies in the occult, (magic rituals) and in economy - money creates power. The Illuminati own all the International banks, the oil-businesses, the most powerful businesses of industry and trade, they infiltrate politics and education and they own most governments - or at the very least control them. They even own Hollywood and the Music Industry.

A good example is the American election for presidency. It is no secret that the candidate who gets the most sponsorship in form of money and positive Media coverage wins the election, as this gives the power to "un-create" the opposed candidate and effectively promote the candidate who will follow the plans of the Illuminati. Media, knowing how to manipulate ignorant people, can easily steer an election in a desired direction so the candidate that's been selected by the Illuminati wins. More often than not, it is the candidate with the 'purest bloodline' and who is the most corrupt that will be chosen for the job. The Illuminati put in top positions people who they know have a dark past, so they can be easily controlled. If these appointed people, who are promised fame and fortune if they follow the rules, are breaking the same rules, the Puppet Masters can easily get them back in line by threatening to put their dirty laundry out to dry in public. If that doesn't help, the person will end up like John F. Kennedy and others.

More often than not the Illuminati sponsors both sides to have a game to entertain the ignorant public. They decide who will be the next president, and they see to that their man wins, even if they have to cheat like they did in Florida when President George W. Bush "won" over Al Gore. Even if their pre-elected candidate for some reason can't win and the other candidate does, they just go to Plan B, which is very well structured and prepared before hand, should this happen. So basically, no matter which candidate wins the race, THEY win. They control both the Democratic and Republican parties. Most President campaigns are financed with drug money, which is understandable when you understand that the Illuminati run the drug trade industry as well. Elections are really not necessary, but they let us vote so we can have a game, and by letting us do so, they pretend to follow the Constitution. It gives us an illusion of choice.

But isn't the President running the game? Not the least. Think of the President as the CEO of big corporate

America. He is the decision maker as long as he is following the polices of the company. If he should have his own ideas how to change things, he needs approval from the real owners of America Inc., which is the Hidden Hand, the Illuminati. The power is not with the politicians, but with the Illuminati, whose top players, as far up in power as we can confirm, are mostly of a Sectarian Jewish Elite, who in modern time use Zionism as a tool to create a Jewish State in Israel with Jerusalem as their Capitol. Zionists are not to be confused with the common Jews, who have nothing to do with this treason against humanity. Soon enough you will see that you don't even have to be a Christian to realize that the Bible Prophecies anticipating an AntiChrist and the "End of the World as we know it" are actually unfolding right before our eyes!

Matthew 19:24 "It is easier for a camel to go through the eye of a needle, than for a rich man to enter the kingdom of God"

-- King James
Bible

Elvis Killed Kennedy
Written by: K. Shah pka Professor Griff

Elvis Killed Kennedy
The 7TH Octave
Title: The Sev7enth Degree
Label: Slam Jamz
Release Date: 1/4/2004

Pre-lude
Back in the days when we established this rock and roll thing
and they give the credit to elvis and kennedy
Listen no need in covering up with a conspiracy

Intro
Not a phrase they even miss
They stole the soul but pick up on this
High powered soul jackers Kennedy in the cross hairs
Silhouette of a man and a king and........ Oh yeah

Verse 1
This is ahhh... APB all points bulletin
It's a must that we have apprehended
One, EAP check the VIP
Every greasy spoon joint, Especially in Tennessee
We got the country on lock
And if you see him yo! just ask him to stop
Drop the accent lose the disguise
The phony pelvic thrust and fake blue eyes

He stole our style and he's known to sweat us
Check every little whore house in Texas
Check Mr. Piggley's Bar and Grill
Take'em alive and don't shoot to kill
I wanna question the bitch smack the bastard
Send him on a trip in a brown paper basket
He left his footprints with his blue suede shoes
On the grassy knoll, the first of six clues
Don't show up on our block, not where we rock,
Not where we live, not where we gig
There's been several sightings, but not confirmed
No longer the other man how quickly we learned
He was there that day I seen him in the grassy knoll
He attempted to speak but the mic he couldn't
hold.....com'on.

Chorus
Cause Elvis Killed Kennedy
Conspiracy
Cause Elvis Killed Kennedy
Conspiracy
Cause Elvis Killed Kennedy
Conspiracy
Cause Elvis Killed Kennedy

Musical Vamp
What's the name of this one..........

Vocal vamp
In the minds of most Americans........Elvis

Verse 2
Stop the press, look who crossed over
Elvis the hound dog, lets stop and think it over
Oswald setup as a patsy and a flunky
It might just have been Elvis up in brick suppository
Doing old ass cover tunes and heavy drinking
Banned from MTV cuz they caught his ass lip-synching
From the belly of the beast Spitting lovely lullabies
Tantalizing loved ones Mothers, lovers and wives...uhhh
Stop it, you're trying to sell sex like six packs
But Elvis flipped the scrip like psychedelic
Ill informed you might have just missed the facts
Missed the real like Chuck Berry did his beats jacked
Don't reverse the message don't confuse the sound
Don't think Little Richard wanted to stay underground
Give respect to where respect is due
No lick line or lyric could ever protect you

Chorus
Cause Elvis Killed Kennedy
Conspiracy
Cause Elvis Killed Kennedy
Conspiracy
Cause Elvis Killed Kennedy
Conspiracy
Cause Elvis Killed Kennedy

Guitar solo....

As the information began to spread among young people over the internet The Black Dot decided to record an album in which I had the pleasure of recording this song. "Rite On" was right in vein with what we were speaking about on the lecture circuit.

Rite On
Written by: K. Shah pka Professor Griff

Heirz to the Shah
Release Date: 2012
(A song I recorded with Black Dot)

This is a message for the angels and the demons
DareDevils are scheming while the chosen ones are really fenin
It's come to my attention, that they fail to mention
Fluoride, chemtrails, h.a.a.r.p and all this mental illness
Turn up the temp, bring the heat to the front line
This is a battle for your head heart soul and mind.
Step up to this on your stairway to heaven
Bloodlines are 13, the god degree is 7
They wiki leak this society secretive
Cloaks oath and baphomet illuminazi cheap trick
In god they lust is on the back of the cash they use
This racist race control the tv and the nightly news
The facts are facts got the masses asses cashless
Eat with the same hand they use to wipe there ass wit
Wake up nah in fact, go the fuck back to sleep
Bad man Griff, spit, n facts it's rated PE

The word about the secret society controlling Hip Hop spread far and wide and I was contacted by a recording artist from Turkey who I wrote a verse to record for his album having these discussions leading to the writing of a few more songs about "The Illuminati's takeover of Hip Hop".

Riots of Rage
Written by: K. Shah pka Professor Griff

Riots of Rage
The 7TH Octave
Title: God Damage
Label: Slam Jamz/Heirz To The Shah
Release Date: 2/1/2011

Face of Satan, IMF and World Banks
Heads Paper chasin, Prison pop they must a inflate
Destruction caution
Dropping those demonic vibes
Violating the minds of silence Illuminati cannot hide
Behave with violence, Skull and Bones global plot
Death of souls, The operation garden plot
Mental battle grounds, Get your mind right
Hood got reasons yo, Elitist power we fight
Silence plot, To pop Pac
The Pope's skirt is up as the missiles drop

Chorus
Like birds in a cage, Riots of rage

Americans are reinforced to believe that individuals are largely in control of their own destiny. Hard work, sacrifice, and personal effort, we are told, determine what happens to us. But increasingly, the fundamental institutions of American society function unfairly, restricting access and opportunity for millions of people.

The greatest example of this is the present-day criminal justice system.

-----By Manning Marable

Resource Information:

The IMF enslavement of Black Africa
http://www.finalcall.com/artman/publish/Perspectives_1/ The_IMF_enslavement_of_Black_Africa_1127.shtml

U.S. Prison Population Hits All-Time High: 2.3 Million Incarcerated
http://abcnews.go.com/TheLaw/story?id=5009270&page =1

Incarceration vs. Education: Reproducing Racism and Poverty in America
http://urbanhabitat.org/node/2808

The Prison Industry In The United States: Big Business Or A New Form Of Slavery?
http://www.november.org/stayinfo/breaking3/GranmaIntl .html

Fluoride - Illness that arise behind the use of fluoride; Big Government conspiracy theories become reality: Fluoride, cancer, chemicals and more
http://www.naturalnews.com/037375_Big_Government_consp iracy_theories_fluoride.html#ixzz2Hh1X4YGI

Some deadly side effects of consuming fluoridated tap water
Wednesday, December 05, 2012 by: J. D. Heyes
http://www.naturalnews.com/038217_fluoride_tap_water
_side_effects.html#ixzz2Hh64TL8T

Yet more studies link fluoride to brain damage
Thursday, September 27, 2012 by: J. D. Heyes;
http://www.naturalnews.com/037339_fluoride_brain_da
mage_studies.html#ixzz2Hh6wcNLJ

Nearly all conventional food crops grown with fluoride-laced water, then sprayed with more fluoride; Monday, September 10, 2012 by: Ethan A. Huff, staff writer.
http://www.naturalnews.com/037138_food_crops_irrigati
on_fluoride.html#ixzz2Hh7UKBJO

History of Medicine Fact #8: U.S. water fluoridation began in 1945 and continues today, despite the fact that the FDA has never approved it; Sunday, June 24, 2012 by: S. D. Wells
www.naturalnews.com036280_history_water_fluoridatio
n_FDA_approval.html#ixzz2Hh88t17H

Astroturf on literal parade: Occupy DC agitator admits to paying protesters.

The Daily Caller has some entertaining video up of a 'Occupy DC organizer' admitting that some of the spontaneous voluntary protesters that he has in tow – ones, not even incidentally, that are more, ah, diverse than the baseline of 'pasty-faced white twenty-something hipster who's seriously underwater in his/her liberal arts degree

student debt' – are actually being paid to show up and wave signs in a language that is perhaps not the mother tongue of the country of their birth*
http://www.redstate.com/2011/10/07/astroturf-on-literal-parade-occupy-dc-agitator-admits-to-paying-protesters/

Chemtrails - Chemtrails are Real; Chemtrails are real and they are damaging our health Wednesday, June 01, 2011 by: Paul Fassa
http://www.naturalnews.com/032572_chemtrails_health.html

Find out how chemtrails adversely affect your health; Wednesday, September 19, 2012 by: Paul Fassa
http://www.naturalnews.com/037239_chemtrails_barium_nanoparticles.html#ixzz2Hh5OrDGi

Chemtrails used for corporate profits, weapons and depopulation agendas
Thursday, October 11, 2012 by: Jonathan Landsman
http://www.naturalnews.com/037498_chemtrails_depopulation_agenda.html#ixzz2Hh9Nj9rD

Denying chemtrails is dangerous for your health
Saturday, March 17, 2012 by: Paul Fassa
http://www.naturalnews.com/035269_chemtrails_asthma_health_effects.html#i
xzz2HhAGfJm9
Eyes Wide Shut: Disease and Death from the Sky; Saturday, June 05, 2010 by: Paul Fassa
http://www.naturalnews.com/028930_chemtrails_chemicals.html#ixzz2HhAhxwfK

Haarp – What is it and its use

The High Frequency Active Auroral Research Program (HAARP) is an ionospheric research program jointly funded by the U.S. Air Force, the U.S. Navy, the University of Alaska, and the Defense Advanced Research Projects Agency (DARPA).[1] (. ^ a b "HAARP Fact Sheet". HAARP. 15 June 2007. Retrieved 27 September 2009.)

http://en.wikipedia.org/wiki/High_Frequency_Active_Au roral_Research_Program

HAARP is a weapon of mass destruction - Radio Waves strong enough to cause earthquakes are controlled by the U.S. military.

http://www.bariumblues.com/haarp1.htm

Bloodlines are 13 – Who are they and what is their role in the World

The 13 Family Bloodlines of the Illuminati: Is the Illuminati Real?

http://kittythedreamer.hubpages.com/hub/The-13-Family-Bloodlines-of-the-Illuminati-Is-the-Illuminati-Real

The Satanic Bloodlines - by: Fritz Springmeier

http://www.theforbiddenknowledge.com/hardtruth/the_sa tanic_bloodlines.htm

BEC - Because the unaware are unaware that they are unaware

http://nwomirror.tripod.com/13bloodlines.html

The 13 Bloodlines That Control The World
http://www.disclose.tv/forum/the-13-bloodlinesthat-control-the-world-t31919.html

Hidden Hand
Interview With Hidden Hand, Alleged Ruling Bloodline Priest
http://www.wanttoknow.info/secret_societies/hidden_han d_bloodlines
IMF – What is it? What is its role? About the IMF (International   Monetary   Fund)
http://www.imf.org/external/about.htm

International Financial Institution;
http://en.wikipedia.org/wiki/World_Bank

Prison Population – Where does the US Rank; Entire world - Prison Population Rates per 100,000 of the national   population
http://www.prisonstudies.org/info/worldbrief/wpb_stats.p hp?area=all&category=wb_poprate

U.S. prison population dwarfs that of other nations - By Adam Lipton
Published: Wednesday, April 23, 2008
http://www.nytimes.com/2008/04/23/world/americas/23i ht-23prison.12253738.html?pagewanted=all&_r=0

What Good Iz a Bomb?
(Poly-Trick; Bloodsuckers of the Poor)

What Good Iz A Bomb?

Polly tricks and the blood suckers of the poor. In defining politics which is many blood suckers, many tics, many tricks I often pull from Elijah Muhammad's lessons *(The Supreme Wisdom)* that he gave us about the (10%) ten percent blood suckers of the poor, which is that ten percent element that's not part of the (5%) five percent who are (PRT) poor righteous teachers of the planet earth and they are not part of the (85%) eighty-five percent who are the blind, deaf and dumb. This (10%) ten percent constitutes the *Illuminati* and once again that same theme running through a different song which I entitled *What Good Iz a Bomb*, which is on my Seventh Degree album that I recorded with my band The 7th Octave. Now this song came out as a result of or came as a result of wanting to experiment with fusions of different music genres like Sly and the Family Stones singing a simple song so when I met Khiry Win, my guitar player in the 7th Octave and now the guitar player in Public Enemy I met him through Eli who was a drumming instructor at Morehouse College. And I often say in reference to people like Eli all musicians are very good musicians but they are not very good people but it came to birth talking about What Good Iz A Bomb and it came to birth and it brought to birth The 7th Octave. Now when I was introduced to rap metal, a new music genre, I instantly fell in love with it simply because it spoke to aspects of who I am as a musician, a writer and an artist. I began to seek out musicians, groups, songs, video footage of groups like Rage Against The Machines, Poppa Roach, Corn, Limp Biscuit. At that particular time I was listening to Rage Against The Machines song 'Calm Like a Bomb' so many times I think it became engrained in the subconscious. Subsequently when you hear What Good Iz A Bomb it may remind you of 'Calm Like A Bomb' but me and Chuck always joked around about can a black man have a bomb and if we did have a bomb what would we do with it? Since the song was so hard I brought power Born in, another vocalist. I brought him in on the song, his government name was Richard Everett. I brought him in, I think, in my opinion he is a very prolific writer and MC surprisingly enough he was one of the first MC's that helped me form the band The 7th Octave. He was out of Savannah, Georgia surprisingly enough DJ Lord, who is the DJ for Public Enemy is out of Savannah, Georgia. Both of these gentlemen were introduced to me, which would ultimately affect my music career. They were introduced to me by a gentleman by the name of Jabhad, who was another MC out of Savannah, Georgia but What Good Iz A Bomb was written and recorded and put on The 7th Octave 1st installment, our first album The 7th Degree.

What Good Iz a Bomb?
Written by: K. Shah pka Professor Griff

What Good Iz A Bomb?
The 7TH Octave
Title: The Sev7enth Degree
Label: Slam Jamz
Release Date: 1/4/2004

I got something to say
About the shit that went down What good iz a Bomb

Chorus 3X
What good iz a Bomb

Disaster strikes as tourist take flicks
Fortunate like society cashless glitch
Found my niche
Got an itch in my index finger
The threat is real now
Who's pointing the finger uuuuh

Spread of Aids I wonder who
World Health organization anti-nigger proof
Check points loose the noose
Violent protest best we stage a coup
This surge of violence came swift and interchangeable
I recognize the retaliation from every angle

Chorus 3X
What good iz a Bomb

Politicians on some big brother shit
The government killed its own they did back in 66
Federal terrorist protect the super rich
Rex 84 and some co-in-tel tricks

Intervention in the affairs of the poor
Who's the hidden hand behind the locked door
Barbaric acts go unpunished
Civil liberties, uuhh they done away with, uuhh
Fake protestors light the fuse
Life or death now which one will you choose

What good iz a bomb
It destroys life
Whether white or black
The 7th Octave yall
Heavy mental in the revolutionary age of heavy metal

"The CIA have done things that will make Hitler blush".
------ Dick Gregory

I got somethin to say
About the shit that went down What good iz a Bomb
What good iz a Bomb 3x's
Disaster strikes as tourist take fits

History of American False Flag Operations

World War I, 1914-1918: A U-boat torpedo hit ocean liner Lusitania near Britain and some 1200 people, including 128 Americans, on board lost their lives. Subsequent investigations revealed that the major explosions were inside the Lusitania, as it was secretly transporting 6 million pounds of artillery shells and rifle ammunition, as well as other explosives on behalf of Morgan banking corporation to help their clients, the Britain and the France. It was against US laws to transport war materials and passengers in the same ship.

War on Terror: The war was launched by Bush administration October 2001. The war was claimed to be the response on terrorism, especially the 9-11 incidents. Most of the people in the world today know that these reasons are false and that those events were based on MIH type (make it happen) inside job.

Fortunate like society cashless glitch
Found my nitch
Got an itch in my index finger
This is dirt is real now
Who's pointin the finger uuuuh
Spread of Aids I wonder who

World Health Organization

(WHO), specialized agency of the United Nations, established in 1948, with its headquarters at Geneva. WHO admits all sovereign states (including those not belonging to the United Nations) to full membership, and it admits territories that are not self-governing to associate membership. There are 192 member nations. WHO is governed by the World Health Assembly, consisting of representatives of the entire membership, which meets at least once a year; an executive board elected by the World Health Assembly; and a secretariat headed by a director-general. There are regional organizations in Africa, the E Mediterranean, SE Asia, Europe, the W Pacific, and the Americas. WHO worked to eradicate smallpox, has made notable strides in checking polio, leprosy, cholera, malaria, and tuberculosis, and sponsors medical research on tropical and other diseases. WHO has drafted conventions for preventing the international spread of disease, such as sanitary and quarantine requirements, and for reducing smoking, and has given attention to the problems of environmental pollution. WHO is also authorized to issue global health alerts and take other measures to prevent the international spread of health threats.

See C. F. Brockington, World Health (1958); M. C. Morgan, Doctors to the World (1958); G. Mikes, The Riches of the Poor: A Journey Round the World Health Organization (1988); P. Wood, ed., World Health Organization; A Brief Summary of Its Work (1989)

The AIDS epidemic among African-Americans in some parts of the United States is as severe as in parts of Africa, according to a report out Tuesday.

Report: Black U.S. AIDS rates rival some African nations "Left Behind - Black America: A Neglected Priority in the Global AIDS" is intended to raise awareness and remind the public that the "AIDS epidemic is not over in America, especially not in Black America," says the report, published by the Black AIDS Institute, an HIV/AIDS think tank focused exclusively on African-Americans.

"AIDS in America today is a black disease," says Phill Wilson, founder and CEO of the institute and himself HIV-positive for 20 years. "2006 CDC data tell us that about half of the just over 1 million Americans living with HIV or AIDS are black."

AIDS was created at Fort McKinley in the U.S.A.

Report reveals that the AIDS virus has been created by the laboratory to reduce the USA world population mainly in Africa (2000 population program of the UN in 1971 for reducing the world population). It was inoculated into 100 million victims in Africa in 1977 by vaccination campaign against Malaria, etc. The yellow fever vaccines that were intentionally infected AIDS. These campaigns genocidal vaccinations have been made by Christian Missionaries and Associations.

It has also been inoculated in over 2,000 American gays in 1978 in a vaccination campaign against Hepatitis B in the Control Center Outbreak (Center for Disease Control) and the New York Blood Center (Operation Trojan Horse (Trojan Horse)). All these revelations have been proven and made available to the public by the FBI as that requires the Freedom of Information Act's records must be made available to the public after 25 years.

In 1974 Henry Kissinger wrote a memorandum on population control and natural resources and food. It states that demographics and the birth rate must be reduced to allow stability in supplier countries of the USA.

I should mention that there has been since a new CIA report in July 2001 on population growth of world population. This demonstrates that this aspect is a major concern for U.S. authorities. Disappearances and suspicious deaths of microbiologists (at least fifteen) discussed elsewhere in the Radio Nova Arté early April 2002, may be related to military research programs on the development of new virus warfare, for the mass destruction. Some epidemics like those of the flu in the United States in early 2001 that have caused many deaths, or the fatal cases of meningitis that occur sporadically in France, must be considered suspect.

The recognition of a "Special Virus Program" of the United States by Dr. Sanders and Senator Nelson is not new. Many scientists suspected a military origin for certain viruses. Dr. Horowitz had also done a remarkable summary. The campaign of Dr. Graves on the Virus Program of the United States on AIDS, have triggered an avalanche of letters directed at members of Congress and an investigation by the General Accounting Service of the United States. $550 million has actually been spent to grow the virus of AIDS/HIV, in accordance with the laws on the population control adopted in secret during the Nixon administration, as determined by Boyd E. Graves against the President of the United States of America, Supreme Court of the United States, Act No. OO-9587. The act requires a "review", a "neutralization" and U.S. apology on AIDS. The $500 million are missing in the center of the current investigation the General Accounting Service of the United States, triggered by James A. Trafficant of Congress from Ohio, July 23, 2001. According to the Head of quality control of BGC, Michael Gryszkowiec, the investigation of this service on the "Special Virus Program", will make the findings of its report towards the end of April 2002. Although the

Supreme Court of the United States denies the requests of the complainants without making any comment, June 4, 2001, Dr. Graves has announced procedures to re-file a claim of apology on AIDS, on behalf of each of innocent victims infected with the AIDS virus.

Population control populations:
I am hardly surprised by this. It suffices to be in possession of some declassified report on population control and population, to understand that uncontrolled population may be a destabilizing factor for the financial but also diplomatic balance of the planet. We can in this case begin questions on statements by Prime Minister Lionel Jospin in January 2000, when he spoke of Family Planning, which has also been accompanied by a television advertising campaign. This term is actually used extensively in the report Kissinger, who believes that it is a necessity for some countries to déviter too rapid growth in countries including raw material suppliers in the USA.

It is interesting to note that during a newscast in early 2002, the UN had said that AIDS had claimed 22 million lives in Africa. I remembered reading somewhere that number, so I searched my archives and found this. The coincidence of the mortality rate and number of vaccinations performed is surprising.
1967/1969: Immunization Measles/smallpox in West and Central Africa: 20/22 million people spread across 20 countries.

Source: William H. Foege, "Centers for Disease Control" (CDC) in Atlanta. "Measle (measles) vaccination in Africa" presentation at the International Conference Pan American Global Health: "The use of vaccines against viral, bacterial or rickettsial in humans", 14-18/12/1970 on page 208.

World cup organization anti-nigger proof
Check points loose the noose
Violent protest fest we stage a coup
This surge of violence came swift and interchangeable
I recognize the retaliation of every angle
Politicians on some big brother shit
The government killed its own back in 66
Federal terrorist protect the super rich Rex 84

The Lowndes County Freedom Organization (LCDO) was established by Stokely Carmichael in Alabama in 1964. This organization later changed its name to the Black Panther Party. In October 1966 Bobby Seale and Huey Newton formed the Black Panther Party (BPP) in Oakland, California. They named the new organization after the emblem adopted by the Lowndes County Freedom Organization.

The Black Panthers were initially formed to protect local communities from police brutality and racism. The group also ran medical clinics and provided free food to school children. Within a couple of years the Black Panthers in Oakland were feeding over 10,000 children every day before they went to school.

Prominent members of the Black Panthers included Stokely Carmichael, H. Rap Brown, Fred Hampton, Fredrika Newton, Eldridge Cleaver, Kathleen Cleaver, David Hilliard, Angela Davis, Bobby Hutton and Elaine Brown.

The Black Panthers had chapters in several major cities and had a membership of over 2,000. Harassed by the police, members became involved in several shoot-outs. This included an exchange of fire between Panthers and the police at Oakland on 28th October, 1967. Huey Newton was wounded and while in hospital was charged with killing a police officer. The following year he was found guilty of voluntary manslaughter.

On 6th April, 1968 eight BPP members, including Eldridge Cleaver, Bobby Hutton and David Hilliard, were traveling in two cars when they were ambushed by the Oakland police. Cleaver and Hutton ran for cover and found themselves in a basement surrounded by police. The building was fired upon for over an hour. When a tear-gas canister was thrown into the basement the two men decided to surrender. Cleaver was wounded in the leg and so Hutton said he would go first. When he left the building with his hands in the air he was shot twelve times by the police and was killed instantly.

In November 1968 Fred Hampton founded the Chicago chapter of the Black Panther Party. He immediately established a community service program. This included the provision of free breakfasts for schoolchildren and a medical clinic that did not charge patients for treatment. Hampton also taught political education classes and instigated a community control of police project.

One of Hampton's greatest achievements was to persuade Chicago's most powerful street gangs to stop fighting against each other. In May 1969 Hampton held a press conference where he announced a nonaggression pact between the gangs and the formation of what he called a "rainbow coalition" (a multiracial alliance of black, Puerto Rican, and poor youths).

The leaders of the Black Panthers were influenced by the ideas expressed by Malcolm X in the final months of his life. The Panthers therefore argued for international working class unity and supported joint action with white revolutionary groups. The Black Panthers eventually developed into a Marxist revolutionary group.

The activities of the Black Panthers came to the attention of J. Edgar Hoover and the FBI. Hoover described the Panthers as "the greatest threat to the internal security of the country" and in November 1968 ordered the FBI to employ "hard-hitting counter-intelligence measures to cripple the Black Panthers".

http://www.spartacus.schoolnet.co.uk/USApantherB.htm

LONDON, July 22 (Reuters) - Rich individuals and their families have as much as $32 trillion of hidden financial assets in offshore tax havens, representing up to $280 billion in lost income tax revenues, according to research published on Sunday. The study estimating the extent of global private financial wealth held in offshore accounts - excluding non-financial assets such as real estate, gold, yachts and racehorses - puts the sum at between $21 and $32 trillion. The research was carried out for pressure group Tax Justice Network, which campaigns against tax havens, by James Henry, former chief economist at consultants McKinsey & Co. He used data from the World Bank, International Monetary Fund, United Nations and central banks. The report also highlights the impact on the balance sheets of 139 developing countries of money held in tax havens by private elites, putting wealth beyond the reach of local tax authorities. The research estimates that since the 1970s, the richest citizens of these 139 countries had amassed $7.3 to $9.3 trillion of "unrecorded offshore wealth" by 2010. Private wealth held offshore represents "a huge black hole in the world economy," Henry said in a statement. (Reporting by Chris Vellacott)

http://www.huffingtonpost.com/2012/07/22/super-rich-offshore-havens_n_1692608.html

Rex 84 and some co-in-tel tricks
Intervention in the affairs of the poor
Who's the hidden hand behind the locked door

This carefully researched and documented book of nearly 500 pages is a must reading for those who wish to know why the major events of the past have happened.

The back cover of The Unseen Hand, gives a summary of its contents.

"It is the contention of the author that the major events of the past, the wars, the depressions and the revolutions, have been planned years in advance by an international conspiracy. This view is called The Conspiratorial View of History, and it is definitely not the view held by the majority of historians today. The more traditional view is called The Accidental View of History, and it holds that no one really knows why events happen—they just do."

"It is the hope of the author that those who read this book will discover that the Conspiratorial View of History is the one best supported by the evidence."

The book is roughly chronological. It starts with early events in history and slowly marches through time until it reaches the 1980's. According to Epperson, the conspiracy began with the formation of the Illuminati on May 1, 1776. The Illuminati, founded by a Bavarian professor named Adam Weishaupt, dedicated itself to overthrowing the old world order of monarchy by adopting ideals of reason. Mankind, through reason, would come to reject religion and nationalism and found a collectivistic society. Ralph Epperson quickly draws links between the Illuminati and later movements such as Marxism and the socialist Fabians. Another aspect of this conspiracy, in close collaboration with the Illuminati and its later incarnations, is that of international banking. The bankers quickly moved to institute central banks in Europe in order to control the population through the manufacture of fiat money (money backed by debt, not gold or silver) and the creation of inflation. The American revolutionary war and the American civil war were attempts by the bankers to weaken the country and institute a central banking system, a goal finally achieved at Jekyll Island in 1913.

No conspiracy book would be complete without a discussion of the Council on Foreign Relations, the Trilateral Commission, the Freemasons, and the Bilderberg group. All four groups are discussed in some depth here. Epperson takes great pains to point out that most of the upper hierarchy in American government are members of these four groups. The goal of these groups, which are funded by foundations set up by banking and oil interests, is to create a "new world order," or a global socialist/communist government ruled by a small oligarchy of wealthy individuals.

http://www.wingtv.net/unseenhand.html

The barbaric acts go unpunished
Civil liberties uuhh they done away with uuhh
Fake protestors light the fuse

COPS ADMIT COPS CAUGHT BEING FAKE
PROTESTERS ARE COPS
What was interesting about this week's agents
provocateurs is that they got caught on video and the video
was immediately seen by hundreds of thousands of people
all around the world and for possibly the first time ever, a
police department has been shamed into admitting that it
plants disguised cops in protest crowds to stir up shit.

http://wonkette.com/293254/cops-admit-cops-caught-
being-fake-protesters-are-cops

Life or death which one will you choose
What good iz a bomb
It destroys life
Whether white or black
The 7th Octave yall
Heavy mental in the revolutionary age of heavy metal

No, I'm not an American. I'm one of the 22 million black
people who are the victims of Americanism. One of the 22
million black people who are the victims of democracy,
nothing but disguised hypocrisy. So, I'm not standing here
speaking to you as an American, or a patriot, or a flag-
saluter, or a flag-waver - no, not I. I'm speaking as a victim
of this American system. And I see America through the
eyes of the victim. I don't see any American dream; I see
an American nightmare.

http://www.famous-speeches-and-speech-topics.info/famous-speeches/malcolm-x-speech-the-ballot-or-the-bullet.htm

---

Resource Information:

Is AIDS a manmade disease?
The enclosed ad describes something called The Strecker Memorandum, a video that purports to show that AIDS is a manmade disease. This sounds like the usual AIDS-conspiracy mumbo jumbo, but it's so well documented it's made me wonder. Can you get to the bottom of it?
— Edna Welthorpe
http://www.straightdope.com/columns/read/941/is-aids-a-manmade-disease

More "evidence" that AIDS is a man-made disease

http://rense.com/general57/manmade.htm

Theory: AIDS is a man-made disease meant to eradicate African Americans and homosexuals. Some theorists also say there is a cure for the disease being withheld by the government.
http://www.conspire.com/aids-is-a-man-made-disease/

In Africa, in 1977, a free vaccination against Smallpox was offered to the Black citizens of the countries with "population problems". The cost was borne by the United States Health Agencies as a "humanitarian gesture". Again, within 5 years, over 60% of the recipients

presented the HIV virus, and, today well over 20 million face death from AIDS.
http://www.threeworldwars.com/more/aids.htm

The Cashless Society Historical and contemporary perspectives on the future of money
http://cashlesssociety.wordpress.com
The Responsibility of Mobile Money Intellectuals
Pros & Cons of Biometrics and a Cashless Society
Read more: http://www.moneycrashers.com/biometrics-cashless-society/#ixzz2Hh6mJ9ym
http://www.moneycrashers.com/biometrics-cashless-society/
http://tina-rekieta.tumblr.com/post/369258361/cashless-society

The Police State is The Real Threat Against America
"If a nation expects to be ignorant and free... it expects what never was and never will be." – Thomas Jefferson

"Our liberty depends on the freedom of the press, and that cannot be limited without being lost." – Thomas Jefferson

"Those who make peaceful revolution impossible will make violent revolution inevitable." – John F. Kennedy

"A nation that is afraid to let its people judge the truth and falsehood in an open market is a nation that is afraid of its people." – John F. Kennedy
http://www.infowars.com/the-police-state-is-the-real-threat-against-america/

Big Brother is Watching
A History of Government Surveillance Programs
http://civilliberty.about.com/od/waronterror/tp/Surveillan
ce-History.htm

KING ALFRED
In the event of widespread and continuing and coordinated racial disturbances in the United States, King Alfred, at the discretion of the President, is to be put into action immediately.
http://www.blackconsciousradio.com/king_alfred_plan.ht
m

Now A Dayz
(Living in the belly of the beast)

Now A Dayz living in the belly of the beast was written from that perspective. Being in America having the experience that America has to offer good but having to experience it from the black perspective, which is not very good. The songs that I wrote later on that would follow Now A Dayz is a testament to exactly what black people go through and what I have been going through as a writer, an author and an artist. Having to write from my perspective and my point of reference. Those songs are Power To The People and Are You Ready For War. Where do I start? I think I would start by saying that Now A Dayz came to birth simply because I ran into an old army buddy by the name of Earl Holder who I was in a band with back in 1979, picture that. The band was called ESP. Earl Holder ended up becoming my business partner in a studio that I still have called HDQTRZ Digital Studios. I began to work with Earl and as we began to catch up and talk about old times we put the studio together and the first project to come out of the studio was Kid Hopperz. It was a project that I was doing along with Sonja Nicole, Drez the Beat Nick, and a few other people. Surprisingly enough, you remember the people Cisco and Ebert? Ebert's daughter, whom I was working with to actually shop this particular project to Hollywood people that had money that could hopefully finance it, nonetheless it never materialized, never took off but I did manage to finish one album – The Fundamentals. Earl Holder ended up producing that out of our studio –HDQTRZ. I got a call from Chuck D, who wanted me to write and produce a song for the Revolverlution album for Public Enemy.

At that time I was working on a children's album entitled "Fundamentals" and the group was an animated concept that I had created called "Kidd Hopperz". Putting the project aside I produced a song called Now A Dayz simply because I was producing a song for children I still experienced what I experienced as a black man in America. This particular song came from that experience. Now A Dayz is a song from my perspective about living in the belly of the beast. As the chorus states Now A Dayz is the ballot or the bullet dealing with the vote. Its your choice you can drop it or you can pull it. Now A Dayz I rep the code of the heat, meaning guns and artillery having to deal with the street but Now A Dayz we need to rest in peace. Now A Dayz talked about the whole gamut of existing living as a black man in America.

NOW A DAYZ
Written by: K. Shah pka Professor Griff

Now A Dayz
Public Enemy
Title: Revolverlution
Label: Slam Jamz
Release Date: 7/23/2002

PE to the PG, enemy of the state, the X Minista
Disparate times call for disparate measures.
Yo! Flav, yo! Chuck, What time is it?

Verse 1
My mental picture distorted by lies
And lie witness news teams scheme up bloody alibis
Selling fake ballots and bullets and wet dreams to a non right teen
I mean shit ain't this the American dream
Can't feed me or seeds need cream
With all due respect dude
You bound to catch a wreck
Rep the struggle with no excuses
Your choice you can choke or you can chose it
This ill-literature is now lit for ya!
Death tones in mono, I mean all those that know, know
The rap game with nigga
Wit niggas who figure pullin triggas to make other niggas bigger niggas
Consciousness is under attack

By those who came to support pro facts, I'm black
Living legend in this game with no toys
Can I be the next vet to bring noise

Chorus 2X
Now a dayz, its the ballot or the bullet
Choice you can drop it, you can pull it
Now a dayz rep the code of the heat
Rest in peace

Verse 2
Time to face the beast of the madness
Over tax'd and stressed to the max I must confess
Rage against the system check
License plate still reads..........Truly blessed
As I manage to lie from paycheck to pay debt
Sons of god rob daughters of a thought process
For your infomaniaxs with number 2 pens in cells
Locked for the true facts they tell
Shit, damn right I'm vex
They building prison industrial complex
My culture is bullet proof
Some of you mother fuckers don't have a got damn clue
You steady stacking government cheese with benefits
Pimps preachin with religious faceless
It won't hurt clench your fist, throw it out
Its now or never click click boom what the fuck!

Chorus 2X
Now a dayz, its the ballet or the bullet

Choice you can drop it, you can pull it
Now a dayz rep the code of the heat
Rest in peace

Musical vamp/Interlude

Rest in peace
Now a dayz all these cats do is bling bling
Different cats but its all about the same thing
Now a dayz its all about being thugged out
For real but the shit is really played out
Now a dayz you can call it what you want
You gettin played or your playin on the corner
And now a dayz its about stayin alive
Now a dayz your either dead or alive
Now A Dayz
Now A Dayz

"Jewish doctors were injecting black babies with AIDS"
*Steve Cokely, 1989 while an aide to Mayor Eugene Sawyer of Chicago
"The AIDS virus had been invented by Jewish doctors to kill black babies".
*Steve Cokely, 1991 on Los Angeles' KPFK-FM, of the Pacifica Radio network.

----Steve Cokely

My mental picture distorted by lies
And lie witness news teams scheme up bloody alibis

Development specialist Dr. J. W. Smith, who is Director of Research for the California-based Institute for Economic Democracy, is even more explicit:

"No society will tolerate it if they knew that they (as a country) were responsible for violently killing 12 to 15 million people since WW II and causing the death of hundreds of millions more their economies were destroyed or those countries were denied the right to restructure to care for their people. Unknown as it is, and recognizing that this has been standard practice throughout colonialism, that is the record of the Western imperial centers of capital from 1945 to 1990... While mouthing peace, freedom, justice, rights, and majority rule, all over the world state-sponsored terrorists were overthrowing democratic governments, installing and protecting dictators, and preventing peace, freedom, justice, rights, and majority rule. Twelve to fifteen million mostly innocent people were slaughtered in that successful 45 year effort to suppress those breaks for economic freedom which were bursting out all over the world... All intelligence agencies have been, and are still in, the business of destabilizing undeveloped countries to maintain their dependency and the flow of the world's natural wealth to powerful nations' industries at a low price and to provide markets for those industries at a high price."

Smith, J. W., 'Simultaneously Suppressing the World's Break for Freedom', *Economic Democracy: The Political Struggle of the Twenty-First Century*, M. E. Sharpe, New York, Armonk, 2000. Excerpts of this study can be found at Institute for Economic Democracy, "http://www.slonet.org/~ied/". In his *Killing*

Hope, former State Department official and investigative journalist William Blum confirms an even larger number of direct deaths than that produced by Smith.

The six corporations that collectively control U.S. media today are Time Warner, Walt Disney, Viacom, Rupert Murdoch's News Corp., CBS Corporation and NBC Universal. Together, the "big six" absolutely dominate news and entertainment in the United States. But even those areas of the media that the "big six" do not completely control are becoming increasingly concentrated. For example, Clear Channel now owns over 1000 radio stations across the United States. Companies like Google, Yahoo and Microsoft are increasingly dominating the Internet.

But it is the "big six" that are the biggest concerns. When you control what Americans watch, hear and read you gain a great deal of control over what they think. They don't call it "programming" for nothing.

Back in 1983 it was bad enough that about 50 corporations dominated U.S. media. But since that time, power over the media has rapidly become concentrated in the hands of fewer and fewer people....

In 1983, fifty corporations dominated most of every mass medium and the biggest media merger in history was a $340 million deal. ... [I]n 1987, the fifty companies had shrunk to twenty-nine. ... [I]n 1990, the twenty-nine had shrunk to twenty three. ... [I]n 1997, the biggest firms numbered ten and involved the $19 billion Disney-ABC deal, at the time the biggest media merger ever. ... [In 2000] AOL Time Warner's $350 billion merged corporation [was] more than 1,000 times larger [than the biggest deal of 1983].

--Ben H. Bagdikian, The Media Monopoly, Sixth Edition, (Beacon Press, 2000), pp. xx—xxi

Selling fake ballots and bullets and wet dreams to a non right teen
I mean shit ain't this the American dream

The term "American dream" is used in many ways, but it essentially is an idea that suggests that anyone in the US can succeed through hard work and has the potential to lead a happy, successful life. Many people have expanded upon or refined the definition to include things such as freedom, fulfillment and meaningful relationships. Someone who manages to achieve his or her version of the American dream is often said to be "living the dream." This concept has been subject to criticism, because some people believe that the structure of society in the US prevents such an idealistic goal for everyone. Critics often point to examples of inequality rooted in class, race, religion and ethnicity that suggest that the American dream is not attainable for everyone.

dream (drēm)

1. a mental phenomenon occurring during REM sleep in which images, emotions, and thoughts are experienced with a sense of reality.

2. to experience such a phenomenon.

dream (dr* m)

A series of images, ideas, emotions, and sensations occurring involuntarily in the mind during certain stages of sleep.

Can't feed me and my seeds need cream
With all due respect dude
You bound to catch a wreck
Rep the struggle with no excuses
Your choice you can choke or you can chose it
This illiterature is now lit for ya!
Death tones in mono, I mean all those that know know
The rap game with nigga
Wit niggas who figure pullin triggas to make other niggas
bigger niggas
Consciousness is under attack
By those who came to support pro facts I'm black
Livin legend in this game with no toys
Can I be the next vet to bring noise
Chorus
Now a dayz, its the ballot or the bullet
Choice you can drop it, you can pull it
Now a dayz rep the code of the heat
Rest in peace

To Whom It May Concern:
Sistar Sekmet
The staff of the Nubian Network
It has been brought to our attention that somebody; a
person, group or organization is calling for the boycott of
certain Black web sites. They are spewing division, venom
and hatred, with some kind of thuggish, jail house

mentality. They are posting their emotional attacks over the Internet, passing around notes and adding childlike remarks to dvd's and cd's every chance they get. We do not know if they are Black, White or Colored, but we do know that they have little information and have no research on the business, situational and political affairs of any of the Black web sites they hope to tear down. The premises of their attacks show no type of class what so ever, are anti-Black and anti-African.

The following list is some of the web sites under attack as far as we presently know: Black Consciousness Online, Sirius Times, LIB Radio Network, Tehuti Online, Black Town, Underground Railroad, The Talking Drum, Black and Noble, Azzaziel Dot Com, Tap Video, Cultural Freedom and Books.

Reality Speaks Media Center, Positively Black, Moorish History and African History on DVD, Inner Light Radio, Africa Within, House of Nubian. http://www.blackconsciousness.com/BoycottScandal.html

Time to face the beast of the madness
Over tax'd and stressed to the max I must confess
Rage against the system check
License plate still reads..........Truly blessed
As I manage to lie from paycheck to pay debt
Sons of god rob daughters of a thought process
For your infomaniaxs with number 2 pens in cells
Locked for the true facts they tell
Shit, damn right I'm vex
They building prison industrial complex
My culture is bullet proof

Some of you mother fuckers don't have a got damn clue
You steady stacking government cheese with benefits

Revelation 13 and Its "Beasts"

The two beasts described in Revelation 13 are among the most enigmatic parts of the book of Revelation, and they have inspired no end of commentary. What is the meaning of these two beasts?

Let's begin by briefly describing what John saw as the first beast. It was a monster having seven heads and ten horns — each with a crown — rising from the sea (verse 1). On each of the beast's heads John saw a name that blasphemed God (verse 2). This beast derived his power and "great authority" (verse 2) from the dragon, who is identified as the devil and Satan (12:8). In fact, the beast was "given authority over every tribe, people, language and nation" — and they worshiped him (verses 7-8).

One of the beast's heads suffered a "fatal" wound from which it was miraculously healed (verse 3). The world was so astonished at this turn of events that it followed the beast. The beast was given authority to exercise his power for 42 months, during which time he was "given power to make war with the saints and to conquer them" (verse 7).

http://www.gci.org/bible/rev/beast

Pimps preachin with religious faceless
It won't hurt clench your fist, throw it out
Its now or never click click boom what the fuck!

Chorus
Rest in peace
Now a dayz all these cats do is bling bling
Different cats but its all about the same thing

Now a dayz its all about being thugged out
For real but the shit is really played out
Now a dayz you can call it what you want
You gettin played or your playin on the corner
And now a dayz its about stayin alive
Now a dayz your either dead or alive
Now A Dayz
Now A Dayz

And they preached another gospel... M-O-N-E-Y!!! Brother Ringo has exposed the prosperity preachers for who they truly are – prosperity pimps!!! Now take a look at another prosperity pimp who makes no bones about the god whom he serves. "Money cometh to me now!" is the chant being repeated over and over and over again by this congregation.

http://thewartburgw

http://www.pimppreacher.com
atch.com/2010/01/06/prosperity-pimps-fleecing-the-flock/

Power To The People
Written by: K. Shah pka Professor Griff

Power to the people
Release Date: 2012

Who stole the soul, along with the revolution
Head check the clench fist, global solution
Take matters in to your own hands
Politrixz are fuct, we want our own land
How many times, you gin trust, fema's lies
Case n point, who care you live or die
Noise n non-sense, in fact kept intact hip hop 5 elements

Prevent the rise of the black messiah
It's bout time to take the people higher n higher
Drugging the citizens and dumbing down the children
Gov't vandals hypocrites and hoodlums
Political targets, CIA crack cocaine nightmares
The murderous, bloodlust, the wealth is not shared
Military extremist, soldier of fortune type
The weekend warriors, war on terrorist hype.

Now don't get me wrong, yo I know it's on
I don't even mine if you sing along (freedom songs)
Plantation politics, the remix is gone
All around the world, not the same ole song

The god of your enemy is not, the god of your friend
Cuz the god of your friend, is not the god in the end

This is some deep sick issssh if I can it myself
Only blind deaf and dumb, not the rich and their wealth
All the lost liberties and UN - souled mysteries
Media viruses and all the world war series

Agents of the oppression, and this spiritual homicide
Psychic phenomenon and castrated mentacide
Chemical warfare, anthraxz and state tax
Useless eaters, native, Latina poor whites and blacks

Drop n facts lets act like we back
Ethnic bombs for Osama and Sadaam
Made for you and I, if we don't get it on
Seize the time, set off this PE'z revolution of the mind.

"We jumped into the protest of Vietnam before the Black Panther Party ever started, before the Black Panther Party was even thought of. In fact, it was late 1965 and 1966 that the anti-Vietnam War, anti-draft to the Vietnam War protest started at University of California, Berkeley."

          ----Bobby Seale

Are You Ready For War
Written by: K. Shah pka Professor Griff

Chorus
Are you ready for war/Are you ready for war
Foreign troops on our sole
Are you ready for war/Are you ready for war
Mentally physically spiritually

Verse 1
We interrupt the corrupt to bring you this broadcast
Global heist n great recession
In the forecast stock market crash
Like Sadaam wit bombs and dot-coms
Everything fine just remain calm
Tyranny relies on obedience from the masses
Foreclosure troubles slash the asses to cashless
What makes people obey the system?
They got that RIDF chip shit all in'em
Hallucinations and near-total amnesia,
Beats and rhymes to educate to free ya, I'll see ya
Transferring power to the State.
Nerve agent antidotes, for hate, that hate the hate
Ron Paul called for a "minding our own business"
That's the business but you ain't wit it, cuz you ain't follow me
Hide the killing of civilians
Not tens but millions
Peep the card of the G.O.D. on guard
For the M15 and KGB n MOSSAD.

They increased military spending
And the defense budget, enuf to kill everyone 10X's fuck
it

Verse 2
The death squads and false Gods
Camps of concentration elf frequencies and amps
No patients hidden in frustration
Yo salvation will keep u on this global plantation
Who's the criminal face of Nato's Rebels don't think
The alpha bet boys won't tell you Al-Qaida mercs
While rappers rock purses and shirts
Like dirt sheets reality show perks
Pentagon shift, Lada's De-Script of the bitch
Un warrantless search it hurts the script
What goes up must come down sound like we got boots on
the ground
Tax revolts and the 08 panic
Nato missiles, aimed at the planet
Iran has a nuke, we got proof from the troops
Violating the rights, the CIA's Global Heist.
Mkultra and mirco chips,
Are you for war against the bitch.

Resource Information:

Lie Witness News Teams - Media
What is the definition of news media

http://reference.yourdictionary.com/word-definitions/what-is-definition-of-news   media.html

Ballots and Bullets – The Vote Scam
The Stealing of America
http://www.votescam.org/

Vote Fraud
http://www.votefraud.org/

The American Dream – What Is The American Dream
The American Dream – Definition
http://en.wikipedia.org/wiki/American_Dream

What is the American Dream
http://www.votefraud.org/

Consciousness Is Under Attack – What is Black Consciousness
Black Consciousness – Definition
http://www.azapo.org.za/links/bcc.htm

United Black America
http://unitedblackamerica.com/definition-black-consciousness/

Sons of God Rob Daughters –
Who Are the Sons of God and Daughters of Men in Genesis 6:1-5? from R.C.   Sproul Jr. Sep 22, 2012
http://www.ligonier.org/blog/who-are-sons-god-and-daughters-men-genesis-6/

Who were the "sons of God" who married "the daughters of men" and had children who were giants in Genesis 6:2-4?

Are these "sons of God" angels, as some have concluded? Can angels reproduce?
http://www.ucg.org/bible-faq/who-were-sons-god-who-married-daughters-men-and-   had-children-who-were-giants-genesis-62-4

Prison Industrial Complex
Prison – Definition
http://en.wikipedia.org/wiki/Prison

What is the difference between a jail and a prison
http://www.wisegeek.org/what-is-the-difference-between-a-jail-and-a-prison.htm Pimps Preachin

The Pimpin Preacher
http://www.forgottenword.org/pimpingpreachers.html

Is Your Pastor More Pimp Or Preacher? Jul 5, 2012 By Fly Ty
http://oldschool1053.com/2956267/is-your-pastor-more-a-pimp-or-preacher/

Revolution
The Revolutionary Movement

http://www.globalsecurity.org/military/world/cuba/move
ment.htm

The Revolutionary Movement – Definition

http://en.wikipedia.org/wiki/Revolutionary_movement

Politrixz

Politics - Definition

http://en.wikipedia.org/wiki/Politics

5 Elements

The Elements of Hip Hop

http://wiki.answers.com/Q/The_5_elements_of_hip_hop

1.MC'ing 2. Dj'ing 3. Breaking 4.Graffiti 5. Knowledge

The Black Messiah

The Rise of the Black Messiah, Racial Profiling and The
New World Order

http://www.assatashakur.org/forum/breaking-down-
understanding-our-enemies/23804-rise-black-messiah-racial-
profiling-new-world-order.html

Political Targets, CIA Crack Cocaine

War on Drugs – Definition

http://en.wikipedia.org/wiki/War_on_Drugs

The War on Drugs - By Claire Suddath Wednesday, Mar.
25,   2009
http://www.time.com/time/world/article/0,8599,1887488,
00.html#ixzz2HoiLHq00

Plantation Politics

http://www.lordlandonline.com/apps/blog/show/prev?from_id=3606404

Blind Deaf and Dumb Our Savior has Arrived: Chapter 11

The Knowledge of God Himself: (Savior's Day, February 26, 1969)

http://www.seventhfam.com/temple/books/our_saviour/saviour11.htm

The following is a reprint of a booklet written to former and current members of the Nation of Islam by Yahoshuah ben Sadic, author of "The Book of Ephraim"

http://maaliks.com/elijah.htm

Chemical Warfare, Anthraxz

Chemical Warfare – Definition

http://en.wikipedia.org/wiki/Chemical_warfare

How Biological and Chemical Warfare Works by Marshall Brain and Susan L. Nasr

A BULLET FOR MY VALENTINE
(A Suicide Letter From the USA to the US)

America wrote this suicide note and then was too cowardly to go through with the deed. These are some of the reasons and a few of the events that lead up to Americas attempted suicide and the actual letter that was found in her blood dripping hand.

A Bullet for My Valentine

Just in a nutshell. When I came up with the concept of this particular song. It was actually a suicide letter written by America's lover to America. The lover was basically telling America to commit suicide. So I'm writing this suicide letter for my lover and basically all I wanted America to do was sign it. For stating all of the facts and all of the things that America has done to black people and if the letter was not signed then I was basically saying in the song I have a bullet for my valentine. I wrote it Valentine's Day and not believing in America's holidays, not having this emotional response and this emotional tie to these pagan heathen holidays. As revolutionaries normally are lonely during holidays or helluva days as we call them. This was just a song that I wrote in response to the whole idea of an unholy day. Holy is something that has not been mixed, diluted or tampered with. So I guess at the end of the day America should sign the letter and here's the bullet with her name on it.

A BULLET FOR MY VALENTINE
Written by: K. Shah pka Professor Griff

A Bullet For My Valentine
The 7TH Octave
Title: God Damage
Label: Slam Jamz/Heirz To The Shah
Release Date: 2/1/2011

Flowers for the dirty deeds
Chocolate thorns you watch and see

Verse 1
How can I state this.....
Blind I play this
One triple five date this
Freedom I've waited
I witness this homicide
No I can't run and hide
I Feel like I wanna cry
Lord don't let me die
How can I state this
With blood on this playlist
With this ring and this name Miss
Try to urn-claim this
How can I stay alive
With thoughts of suicide
Borders I'm trapped inside
I'm free in my own mind

Bridge/Vamp
Diamonds and genocide
You say you care but you keep me blind
You know what you feel inside
And for this you have to die

Chorus
Flowers for the dirty deed
Chocolate thorns you wait and see
A bullet for my valentine
Flowers for the dirty deed
Chocolate thorns you wait and see
The devil deeds are on time
Flowers for the dirty deed
Chocolate thorns you wait and see
A bullet for my valentine
Flowers for the dirty deed
She Loves to hate my heart and mind

Musical Vamp

Verse 2
How can I believe this
Her death is the evidence
Selfish desires
All hell and not heaven sent
Tears in the eyes
All the deception and lies
I swear I don't know why
Why you speak when you lie

I try to escape this
Nonsense I hate this
From white to black I painted this
You should be ashamed of this
You can't mask the scars
With the beauty that's ours
You live in this evil life filled with stress and strife
If you know what I know you would just let me go
To a love of my own
Cuz I dont feel at home
We must state the facts
To put the life back on track
The knife in the back
I love you you act

Vamp
Diamonds and genocide
You say you care but you keep me blind
You know what you feel inside
And for this you have to die

Guitar solo

Chorus
Flowers for the dirty deed
Chocolate thorns you wait and see
A bullet for my valentine

Flowers for the dirty deed
Chocolate thorns you wait and see

Devils deeds is out of time

Musical Vamp

Bridge
Diamonds and genocide
You say you care but you keep me blind
You know what you feel inside
And for this you have to die

"I believe that it is possible that Jonestown may have been a mind-control experiment. Leo Ryan's congressional visit pierced that cell and would have resulted in its exposure and that our government, or its agent the CIA, deemed it necessary to wipe out over nine hundred American citizens to protect the secrecy of the operation."
* Leo Ryan's aide Joseph Holsinger, 1980 lecture Election Fraud

-----Leo Ryan

This letter was found in any place you might find a suicide note. The words "open upon my death" was written across the front in a very old English cursive style penmanship. The blood stains on the envelope spoke to the nature of the crime that had taken place. As the search for the body ensued, America was nowhere to be found. As I opened the letter it read *"Flowers for the dirty deeds, Chocolate thorns you watch and see"*.

In the 1st verse of the song I made significant references to the in-ability to say *"How can I state this"* because of fear to put my pain and anger, in the bastard language of the enemy hoping that my people hear me. I thought maybe if I attempted to do as others did by protesting and marching the world would know the pain I feel inside and inside of the belly of the beast, America. *"Blind I played this"* not knowing what the out come would be I threw the black power fist in the air wanting someone to unite with me to feel my hurt. "One triple five date this" Writing in a mathematical code I embedded the date of my capture (kid-knapping) and journey to Amerikkka "1555". *"Freedom I waited" "I witness this homicide"* Witnessing the brutality in America of the millions of Africans brought to these shores in chains in the holes of ships. *"No I can't run and hide"* with no escape I'm traumatized by the brutality and devilishment of a people who force their godless culture down my throat. "Feel like I wanna cry" knowing that my screams would go un-heard I chose to sing in the only language I was allowed to use. I found refuge in the blackness of night and the blackness in the black keys on the piano while having my mother and sister raped as I played sweet songs for the white slave master.

"Lord don't let me die" as this life became unbearable, I cried out to the only GOD I was allowed to cry out to, "Jesus". *"How can I fake this"* I never knew this before now but my GOD would never allow such inhumane treatment of a people insync with what appeared to be his will. *"With blood on this playlist"* as Bessie Smith said *"There were strange fruit, with blood at the root."* Every song I could think of to get me through the day reminded me of my souljourn in Amerikkka. *"Ring and this name Miss"* Now married to a alien way acting against the self I accepted names, gods, religions and culture that was

opposite of what I am and what I often thought would cause the death of my soul. *"Try to un-claim this"* as I attempted to hide myself in their culture I managed to lose more and more of who I really am. *"How can I stay alive"* I know that if I reach back to the very Orisias and dieties that have got me through till this point I would be fine, so hide them in the songs that the slave trader would allow us to sing cuz *"A happy nigger is a hard working nigger"*. *"With thoughts of suicide"* My mother wanting to kill herself because she had the child of the slave master growing in her, due to the constant raping of African women *"Borders I'm trapped inside"*. "I'm free in my own mind". She knew she was trapped. The only place we would be free is in our minds and spirit.

Vamp/Bridge
Diamonds and genocide
You say you care
But you keep me blind
You know what you feel inside
And for this you have to die.

Hook/Chorus
Flowers for the dirty deed
Chocolate thorns you wait and see

A bullet for my valentine
Flowers for the dirty deed
Chocolate thorns you wait and see
The devil deeds are out of time

Flowers for the dirty deed

Chocolate thorns you wait and see

A bullet for my valentine

Flowers for the dirty deed
She loves to hate my heart and mind

"How can I believe this; her death is the evidence" The only way we would know that America has repented for what's been done to the black man and woman in America is if the body has been found and the evidence has been processed. *"Selfish desires are hell and not heaven sent".* The riches that have come to America have only come by the theft and rape of the indigenous people of the world. *"Tears in the eyes all the deception and lies swear, don't know why, why you speak when you lie"* The scripture says in the book of John 8:44 Ye are of your father the devil, and the lusts of your father ye will do. He was a murderer from the beginning, and abode not in the truth, because there is no truth in him. When he speaketh a lie, he speaketh of his own: for he is a liar, and the father of it.

"I try to escape this, nonsense I hate this" *"White to black I painted this you should be ashamed of this"* All of those writers who came before me and put it down in black and white all have aspects of the same story, such writers like Fredrick Douglas, "What To The Slave Is The 4th Of July?" FREDERICK DOUGLASS SPEECH, 1852, Independence Day Speech in Rochester, New York Frederick Douglass (A former slave himself, he became a leader in the 19th Century Abolitionist Movement). If there is no struggle, there is no progress. Those who profess to favor freedom, and yet depreciate agitation, are men who want crops without plowing up the ground. They

want rain without thunder and lightning. They want the ocean without the awful roar of its many waters. This struggle may be a moral one; or it may be a physical one; or it may be both moral and physical; but it must be a struggle. Power concedes nothing without a demand. It never did and it never will. The white man's happiness cannot be purchased by the black man's misery. *"Can't mask the scars, with the beauty that's ours"* We are the face of the Statue of Liberty, American's 151-foot-tall monument to freedom erected in New York Harbor in 1886. The traditional view, as taught to American schoolchildren for the past hundred years, holds that Lady Liberty was created to commemorate the friendship forged between the United States and France during the Revolutionary War. By 1903, when the statue was inscribed with Emma Lazarus's poetic words, "Give me your tired, your poor, your huddled masses yearning to breathe free," it had come to symbolize America's status as a safe haven for refugees and immigrants from every corner of the world. During my visit to France I saw the original Statue of Liberty. However there was a difference, the statue in France is Black. The Statue of Liberty was originally a Black woman, but, as memory serves, it was because the model was Black.

In a book called "The Journey of The Songhai People", according to Dr. Jim Haskins, a member of the National Education Advisory Committee of the Liberty-Ellis Island Committee, Professor of English at the University of Florida, and prolific Black author, points out that what stimulated the original idea for that 151 foot statue in the harbor.

He says that what stimulated the idea for the creation of the statue initially was the part that Black soldiers played in the ending of Black African Bondage in the United States. It was created in the mind of the French historian Edourd de Laboulaye, chairman of the French Anti-Slavery Society, who, together with sculptor Frederic Auguste Bartholdi, proposed to the French government that the people of France present to the people of the United States through the American Abolitionist Society, the gift of a Statue of Liberty in recognition of the fact that Black soldiers won the Civil War in the United States. Documents of Proof:

1.) You may go and see the original model of the Statue of Liberty, with the broken chains at her feet and in her left hand. Go to the Museum of the City of NY, Fifth Avenue and 103rd Street write to Peter Simmons and he can send you some documentation.

2.) Check with the N.Y. Times magazine, part II_May 18, 1986. Read the article by Laboulaye.

3.) The dark original face of the Statue of Liberty can be seen in the N.Y. Post, June 17, 1986, also the Post stated the reason for the broken chains at her feet. http://urbanlegends.about.com/library/weekly/aa020900a. htm

You living this evil life, filled with stress and strife

As the reality of slavery in the North faded, and a strident anti-Southern abolitionism arose there, the memory of Northern slaves, when it surfaced at all, tended to focus on how happy and well-treated they had been, in terms much reminiscent of the so-called "Lost Cause" literature that followed the fall of the Confederacy in 1865.

America will continue to live in denial and drown in her pathology through "Color blind denial". "The slaves in Massachusetts were treated with almost parental kindness. They were incorporated into the family, and each puritan household being a sort of religious structure, the relative duties of master and servant were clearly defined. No doubt the severest and longest task fell to the slave, but in the household of the farmer or artisan, the master and the mistress shared it, and when it was finished, the white and the black, like the feudal chief and his household servant, sat down to the same table, and shared the same viands." [Reminiscence by Catharine Sedgwick (1789-1867) of Stockbridge, Mass.]

Yet the petitions for freedom from New England and Mid-Atlantic blacks, and the numbers in which they ran off from their masters to the British during the Revolution, suggest rather a different picture.

"If You know what I know, You'll just let me go" the book of Genesis 15:13 King James Bible (Cambridge Ed.) And he said unto Abram, Know of a surety that thy seed shall be a stranger in a land that is not theirs, and shall serve them; and they shall afflict them four hundred years; clearly states........"To a love of my own, Cause I don't feel at home" Our good Brother Marcus Garvey wanted to go back to Africa. "If You Believe the Negro Has a Soul": "Back to Africa" with Marcus Garvey.

Black Nationalist Marcus Garvey recognized that his Universal Negro Improvement Association (UNIA) would find its most enthusiastic audience in the United States, despite the organization's professed worldwide mission. After fighting World War I, ostensibly to defend democracy and self-determination, thousands of African-

American soldiers returned home to find intensified discrimination, segregation, racial violence, and hostile relations with white Americans. Sensing growing frustration, Garvey used his considerable charisma to attract thousands of disillusioned black working-class and lower middle-class followers and became the most popular black leader in America in the early 1920s. The UNIA, committed to notions of racial purity and separatism, insisted that salvation for African Americans meant building an autonomous, black-led nation in Africa. To this end, the movement offered in its "Back to Africa" campaign a powerful message of black pride and economic self-sufficiency. In Garvey's 1921 speech, "If You Believe the Negro Has a Soul," he emphasized the inevitability of racial antagonism and the hopelessness of interracial coexistence, Marcus Garvey: Fellow citizens of Africa, I greet you in the name of the Universal Negro Improvement Association and African Communities League of the World. You may ask, "what organization is that?" It is for me to inform you that the Universal Negro Improvement Association is an organization that seeks to unite, into one solid body, the four hundred million Negroes in the world. To link up the fifty-million Negroes in the United States of America, with the twenty-million Negroes of the West Indies, the forty-million Negroes of South and Central America, with the two hundred and eighty million Negroes of Africa, for the purpose of bettering our industrial, commercial, educational, social, and political conditions. As you are aware, the world in which we live today is divided into separate race groups and distinct nationalities. Each race and each nationality is endeavoring to work out its own destiny, to the exclusion of other races and other nationalities. We hear the cry of "England for the Englishman," of "France for the Frenchman," of "Germany for the German," of "Ireland for the Irish," of "Palestine for the Jew," of "Japan for the Japanese," of

"China for the Chinese." We of the Universal Negro Improvement Association are raising the cry of "Africa for the Africans," those at home and those abroad. There are 400 million Africans in the world who have Negro blood coursing through their veins, and we believe that the time has come to unite these 400 million people toward the one common purpose of bettering their condition. The great problem of the Negro for the last 500 years has been that of disunity. No one or no organization ever succeeded in uniting the Negro race. But within the last four years, the Universal Negro Improvement Association has worked wonders. It is bringing together in one fold four million organized Negroes who are scattered in all parts of the world. Here in the 48 States of the American Union, all the West Indies islands, and the countries of South and Central America and Africa. These four million people are working to convert the rest of the four hundred million that are all over the world, and it is for this purpose, that we are asking you to join our land and to do the best you can to help us to bring about an emancipated race. If anything state worthy is to be done, it must be done through unity, and it is for that reason that the Universal Negro Improvement Association calls upon every Negro in the United States to rally to this standard. We want to unite the Negro race in this country. We want every Negro to work for one common object, that of building a nation of his own on the great continent of Africa. That all Negroes all over the world are working for the establishment of a government in Africa, means that it will be realized in another few years. We want the moral and financial support of every Negro to make this dream a possibility. Our race, this organization, has established itself in Nigeria, West Africa, and it endeavors to do all possible to develop that Negro country to become a great industrial and commercial commonwealth. Pioneers have been sent by this organization to Nigeria, and they are now laying the foundations upon which the four hundred million Negroes of the world will build. If you believe that the Negro has a soul, if you believe that the Negro is a man, if you believe the Negro was endowed with the senses commonly given to other men by the Creator, then you must acknowledge that what other men have done, Negroes can do. We want to build up cities, nations, governments, industries of our own in Africa, so that we will be able to have a chance to rise from the lowest to the highest position in the African Commonwealth.

We must state the facts to put the life back on track
the knife in the back
I love you act
Diamonds and genocide
You say you care but you keep me blind
You know what you feel inside
And for this you have to die
Flowers for the dirty deeds, chocolate thorns you wait and see
A bullet for my valentine
Flowers for the dirty deeds
Chocolate thorns you wait and see
The devil deeds are out of time

S1W'S TAKEN ON A ROOFTOP IN LA

Source: Courtesy of the Marcus Garvey and the UNIA
Papers Project at the University of California, Los
Angeles. Recording courtesy of Michigan State
University, G. Robert Vincent Voice Library.
http://historymatters.gmu.edu/d/5124

PROFESSOR GRIFF @ 9:30 CLUB IN WASHINGTON, DC 2012

PROFESSOR GRIFF, CHUCK D AND BROTHER MIKE

PROFESSOR GRIFF IN MEDITATION STATE @ 9:30
CLUB IN WASHINGTON, DC 2012

FLAVA FLAV AND PROFESSOR GRIFF

PROFESSOR GRIFF IN HIS KUNG-FU STANCE IN LA

2012 HIP HOP GODS TOUR

WAR CRY

(The Quiet Storm, Hurricane Katrina)

War Cry

The War Cry was a concept I came up with regarding what I was feeling as a result of watching and hearing through the African grapevine what happened to our people during Hurricane Katrina. As I sat back watching the TV literally crying and watching people suffering and dying I picked up the pen and pad and wrote the verse to War Cry and saved it for years before I actually put it down in this song. It actually was really just some notes on a paper expressing how I felt about Hurricane Katrina. If you listen to the verse it actually talks about some of the aspects of Hurricane Katrina which weren't even told during that particular crisis that went down with black people.

To go over it line by line because there are some things I talk about. The Red Cross is white obviously. The black water were the mercenaries that were there shooting black people in the back. They found graves, mass graves of black people. When the water hit there were black men still trapped in prison cells drowning to death. Women were having babies on the bridge handing their babies to strangers never to see their babies again. So many things were going on. I mention MAAFA21. I mention in the first line it was an American tragedy sadly that you thought you would be an American opposed to an African American. Even after all of that you are still black as gladly as matter of factly. Stating truths about what was happening during Hurricane Katrina. A lot of truths as I said that were unknown to the masses of the people especially black people. The media is controlling.

War Cry

Written by: K. Shah pka Professor Griff

War Cry
The 7TH Octave
Title: God Damage
Label: Slam Jamz/Heirz To The Shah
Release Date: 2/1/2011

Verse
American tragedy
Sadly now you're a refugee
African, thought you were an American
Now you don't wanna be
Black as gladly as a matter of factly
Can't understand slow response the white cross is red
obviously
Twisted system like, twisted sista
Battle of a Cajun town and no one missed her
Politicians steppin over helpless victims
They shift the blame and we struggle through the pain
Fight to stay alive we might as well save some lives
Maafa 21, right, 9th ward homicide
Black water, creepin through the mist of the fog on the hills
of the hip hop gods

Bridge
A twisted nation warped by twisted lies
Lies fuel the fears and tears back to lies
Who can deny the crimes that lead to more lies
War crimes war cry

Chorus

hey yah, hey yah, hey yah, hey yah, hey yah, hey yah, hey yah, hey yah,

hey yah, hey yah, hey yah, hey yah, hey yah, hey yah, hey yah, hey yah

---

*"Brownie, you're doing a heckuva job." -- President Bush, Sept. 2. One of the most idiotic, misguided, clueless and smug things the president has said during his two terms in office.

"We ask black people: it's time. It's time for us to come together. It's time for us to rebuild a New Orleans, the one that should be a chocolate New Orleans. And I don't care what people are saying Uptown or wherever they are. This city will be chocolate at the end of the day."

--New Orleans Mayor Ray Nagin, Jan. 16, 2006

American tragedy

Sadly now you're a refugee

African, thought you were an American

Now you don't wanna be

Black as gladly as a matter of factly

Can't understand slow response the white cross is red obviously

The Red Cross of Constantine is officially The Masonic and Military Order of the Red Cross of Constantine and the Orders of the Holy Sepulchre and St. John the Evangelist, the latter two of which are called the Appendant Orders. There are also two chair degrees conferred on the Viceroy and Sovereign of a Conclave, and two honorary orders: Knight Commander of Constantine and Knight Grand Cross. The governing body of the Order for the United States of America, the Republic of Mexico and the Republic of the Philippines and their territories is styled The United Grand Imperial Council of Knights of the Red Cross of Constantine and Appendant Orders for the United States of America, Mexico and the Philippines.

The purpose of the Constantinian Orders are to commemorate the first elevation of Christianity from the position of a despised and proscribed heresy to that of a legally recognized and honored religion, to cultivate the social virtues, appeal to the intellectual and moral qualities, preserve as far as possible the customs of the fraternity and bring about good fellowship and understanding between all branches of Masonry.

Knights Companions of the Order meet in Conclaves of the Red Cross of Constantine and a member must be a Royal Arch Mason in good standing and subscribe to a belief in the Christian religion as revealed in the New Testament. Membership is by invitation and each Conclave has a prescribed membership limit.

Twisted system like, twisted sista
Battle of a Cajun town and no one missed her
Politicians steppin over helpless victims
They shift the blame and we struggle through the pain
fight to stay alive we might as well save some lives
Maafa 21, right, 9th ward homicide

There was a very strong moral worldview with some strong Christian content as well as some strong humanist perspectives; no foul language; discussions of violence, including abortion; discussions of sex; no nudity; no alcohol; no smoking; and, a strong Christian sermon in the end but several references to class warfare.

Summary:

MAAFA 21 is a very carefully reasoned, well-produced exposé of the abortion industry, racism and eugenics. It proves through innumerable sources that many founders of Planned Parenthood and other parts of the abortion movement were interested in killing off the black race in America and elsewhere.

Review:

MAAFA 21 is a very carefully reasoned, well-produced exposé of the abortion industry, racism and eugenics.

Subtitled "Black Genocide in the 21st Century," this video traces the abortion industry back through its eugenics roots. It proves through innumerable sources that the founders of Planned Parenthood and other parts of the abortion movement were interested in killing off the black race in America and elsewhere. The movie exposes some of the most powerful leaders of the socialist and humanist movements of the 20th Century as some of the worst racists, on the same level as Adolf Hitler but much more clever. The argument is presented so well here that it is irrefutable. The taped excerpt of President Nixon saying "kill the black b*st*rds" is horrifying. The filmmakers behind this video calculate that abortion has reduced the black population in the United States by about 25%!

Although MAAFA 21 could be condensed, the filmmakers are clearly interested in getting all the evidence on the table. If this movie gets wide circulation among the

African American community, it should bring an end to Planned Parenthood and the abortion industry.

The only problem with this documentary is that there are several references that sound like class warfare. These are balanced by a good Christian sermon at the end, but it would have been better if it had a coherent Judeo-Christian worldview toward the topic without the accusations of elitism.

That said, clearly the people perpetrating this abortion genocide are elitist in their own minds, and they need to be called to account. MAAFA 21 is a must viewing for every adult in the world whatever their race!

Black water, creepin through the mist of the fog on the hills of the hip hop gods

Blackwater USA is comprised of five companies; Blackwater Training Center, Blackwater Target Systems, Blackwater Security Consulting, Blackwater Canine, and Blackwater Air (AWS). We have established a global presence and provide training and tactical solutions for the 21st century.

Our clients include federal law enforcement agencies, the Department of Defense, Department of State, and Department of Transportation, local and state entities from around the country, multi-national corporations, and friendly nations from all over the globe. We customize and execute solutions for our clients to help keep them at the level of readiness required to meet today's law enforcement, homeland security, and defense challenges. Any and all defense services supplied to foreign nationals will only be pursuant to proper authorization by the Department of State.

Officially, Blackwater says its forces are in New Orleans to "join the Hurricane Relief Effort." A statement on the company's website, dated September 1, advertises airlift services, security services and crowd control. The company, according to news reports, has since begun taking private contracts to guard hotels, businesses and other properties. But what has not been publicly acknowledged is the claim, made to us by 2 Blackwater mercenaries, that they are actually engaged in general law enforcement activities including "securing neighborhoods" and "confronting criminals."

Bridge
A twisted nation warped by twisted lies
Lies fuel the fears and tears back to lies
Who can deny the crimes that lead to more lies
War crimes war cry
Chorus
hey yah, hey yah, hey yah, hey yah, hey yah, hey yah, hey yah, hey yah,
hey yah, hey yah, hey yah, hey yah, hey yah, hey yah, hey yah, hey yah

Touch
Written by: K. Shah pka Professor Griff

Title: God Damage
Label: Slam Jamz/Heirz To The Shah
Release Date: 2/1/2011

You may choose life or death
Choke or gasp for your last breath
Debt or death
Or better yet you satan the devil can have group sex
Hip hop still got beats to death
Passive pussy's question my motives
I'm a local maniac with local motives
Who ducks when the pendulum swings
When the fat lady sings
You measure success by doses, hoses and posters
Or corner blocks posting
One thousand GOD U'S in two thousand palms
Still not convinced turn to the 23rd book of Psalms

"Silence is argument carried out by other means."
                                        ----Che Guevara

RE-NIG

Written by: K. Shah pka Professor Griff

The 7TH Octave
Title: God Damage
Label: Slam Jamz/Heirz To The Shah
Release Date: 2/1/2011

I'm on the peace side of things
Enough to bring my A game to the ning
Now you force me to sing
My pro black is spiritual
Here to spit at you
Meet you in a dark alley
Hypocrites dead rally
The grand composer, great architect
52 card holder, Unstack the deck
Is it the cause of the greed, Lust of the greed
They play the same card twice, use the gun or the mic
Lets sum it up, Traders got it fucked up
Same initials, government officials

A bumper sticker that read: 2012 Don't Re-Nig.

As the great satirist Randy Newman sings in a new satirical ballad: "I'm dreaming of a white president "Just like the ones we've always had "A real live white man who knows the score "How to handle money or start a war." But for others of us, it's not anything so nuanced as a sense of dislocation -- just the same old hate as always.

All is Fair in Love And War

All is fair in love and war
By: Professor Griff

I think in block letters, deep by default fetish
Complexed like reddish, brown Blackfut warrior feathers
I'm living dark matter, evidence, pause the Willie lynch chip, brain splatter
Tanner than, as salaam alaikum
Truth be told, my duracell is 7.5
I think rightly, I'm lefty with right vibes, in my right mind
Put it all On my first born, no lie.
I take, fragments of wasted wisdom
Mixed with, ism and shades thru acashic prisons
The alpha, bet you got a curse on the tongue
Before the next nig at the end of noose get dumb
Krst the crown chakra, UN clog ur hip hop heavy mental soul blocker
I'm the either bender, God body 3rd dimensional black male gender
Scripturelous scripture, Return to sender,
Support the alchemical black light vendors
The emerald tablet, they fuze, demonic, gadgets and fragments.
Got the Pineal Stagnant
100 minus the 85delete the 10% blood suckin lie
UN holy chit chatter,
Badder than mom duke, back when she was a bad mame ma jammer

A style like miles, with a scent of Pachoulli
I'll never let the divine evil rule me

"All is fair in love and war but the soul will cost your more"

Resource Information:

African – Definition
http://en.wikipedia.org/wiki/African_people

African American – Definition
http://en.wikipedia.org/wiki/African_American

American - Definition
http://en.wikipedia.org/wiki/Americans

When Did African Americans Gain Citizenship?
http://wiki.answers.com/Q/When_did_AfricanAmericans
_gain_citizenship_status#

Is the Red Cross a Secret Society or part of the Free Masons?
http://anewdayoutreach.com/kingdomcome.htm

FreeMasons Control the World
http://www.theforbiddenknowledge.com/hardtruth/freem
asons_control_world.htm

Who Are Black Water?
Blackwater's Black Ops - Jeremy Scahill - September 15, 2010
http://www.thenation.com/article/154739/blackwaters-black-ops#

Blackwater-The World's Most Deadly Mercenary Army-
An Interview w/ Jeremy Scahill
http://hiphopandpolitics.wordpress.com/2009/09/02/black
water-the-worlds-most-deadly-mercenary-army-an-
interview-w-jeremy-scahill/

Tyranny – Definition
http://dictionary.reference.com/browse/tyranny

Principles of Tyranny - by Jon Roland
http://constitution.org/tyr/prin_tyr.htm

RFID Chip
Radio-Frequency Chip – Definition
http://en.wikipedia.org/wiki/Radio-
frequency_identification

How RFID Works - by Kevin Bonsor and Wesley Fenlon
http://electronics.howstuffworks.com/gadgets/high-tech-
gadgets/rfid.htm

Nerve Agent Antidotes
Nerve Agent – Definition
http://en.wikipedia.org/wiki/Nerve_agent

Nerve Agents
http://www.opcw.org/about-chemical-weapons/types-of-
chemical-agent/nerve-agents/

MI5 and KGB, MOSSAD
MI5 – Military Intelligence Section 5 – Definition

http://en.wikipedia.org/wiki/MI5

Komitet gosudarstvennoy bezopasnosti or Committee for State Security – Definition
http://en.wikipedia.org/wiki/KGB

MOSSAD -HaMossad leModi'in uleTafkidim Meyuḥadim meaning "Institute for Intelligence and Special Operations
http://en.wikipedia.org/wiki/Mossad

Camps of Concentration
List of Concentration Camps
http://en.wikipedia.org/wiki/List_of_Nazi_concentration_camps

Concentration Camps – Definition
http://www.jewishvirtuallibrary.org/jsource/Holocaust/whatarecamps.html

Elf Frequencies
Extremely Low Frequencies – Definition
http://en.wikipedia.org/wiki/Extremely_low_frequency

Biohazards of Extremely Low Frequencies (ELF) - by Dr. Nick Begich
http://www.earthpulse.com/src/subcategory.asp?catid=1&subcatid=4

Alpha Bet Boys (FBI, CIA, FCC, ATF)
Federal Bureau of Investigation – Definition

http://en.wikipedia.org/wiki/Federal_Bureau_of_Investig
ation

Central Intelligence Agency – Definition
http://en.wikipedia.org/wiki/Central_Intelligence_Agency

Federal Communications Commission - Definition
http://en.wikipedia.org/wiki/Federal_Communications_C
ommission

Bureau of Alcohol, Tobacco, Firearms and Explosives -
Definition
http://en.wikipedia.org/wiki/Bureau_of_Alcohol,_Tobacc
o,_Firearms_and_Explosives

Warrantless Search
Warrantless Search – Definition
http://en.wikipedia.org/wiki/Warrantless_searches_in_the
_United_States

What Is Probable Cause for a Warrantless Search? By
Cindy Hill, eHow Contributor
http://www.ehow.com/about_5412328_probable-cause-
warrantless-search.html#ixzz2Hp0W02HI
NATO
North Atlantic Treaty Organization – Definition
http://en.wikipedia.org/wiki/NATO

NATO Member Countries
http://www.nato.int/cps/en/natolive/nato_countries.htm

Who are the 5 Percenters?
http://www.answering-islam.org/Index/F/five_percenters.html

Nation of Gods and Earths/Five Percent FAQ (frequently asked questions)
http://www.blackapologetics.com/fivepercentfaq.html

The GODS Of Hip-Hop: A Reflection On The Five Percenter Influence On Rap Music & Culture - by Dasun Allah March 24, 2010

http://hiphopwired.com/2010/03/24/the-gods-of-hip-hop-a-reflection-on-the-five-percenter-influence-on-rap-music-culture/#M9M0Pvr2cEM8DCeA.99

23rd Book Of Psalms
http://www.worldprayer.us/bible/B19C023.php4
The Lord is my Shepherd; I shall not want.
He maketh me to lie down in green pastures:
He leadeth me beside the still waters.
He restoreth my soul:
He leadeth me in the paths of righteousness for His name' sake.
Yea, though I walk through the valley of the shadow of death,
I will fear no evil: For thou art with me;
Thy rod and thy staff, they comfort me.
Thou preparest a table before me in the presence of mine enemies;
Thou annointest my head with oil; My cup runneth over.

Surely goodness and mercy shall follow me all the days of my life,

And I will dwell in the House of the Lord forever.

---KJV

Blackfut – Who are the Blackfoot tribe

Blackfeet Indian History

http://www.accessgenealogy.com/native/tribes/blackfeet/blackfeetindiantribe.htm

Black Foot Confederacy – Definition

http://en.wikipedia.org/wiki/Blackfoot_Confederacy

Native Languages of the Americas: Blackfoot (Siksika, Peigan, Piegan, Kainai, Blackfeet) http://www.native-languages.org/blackfoot.htm

Dark Matter

Dark Matter – Definition

http://en.wikipedia.org/wiki/Dark_matter

What does "dark matter" mean?

http://www.scienzagiovane.unibo.it/english/darkmatter/1-dark-mean.html

Willie Lynch Chip

How to Deactivate Your Willie Lynch Chip

http://blackhistoryfactorfiction.com/?p=4427#

How to Deactivate Your Willie Lynch Chip vs. Death of the Willie Lynch Speech http://ebookbrowse.com/how-to-deactivate-the-willie-lynch-chip-vs-death-of-the-willie-lynch-speech-pdf-d247708662

Willie Lynch Speech
http://en.wikipedia.org/wiki/William_Lynch_speech

Akashic – what is the akashic records
Akashic Records – Definition
http://en.wikipedia.org/wiki/Akashic_records
WHAT ARE THE AKASHIC RECORDS? by Dr. Daniel
Condron
http://www.som.org/9intuition/akashicrecords.htm
Why Access The Akashic Records?
http://www.soulrealignment.com/akashic-records/#

Crown Chakra
Crown Chaka – Definition
http://crystal-cure.com/chakra-crown.html

Energy Healing and Spiritual Healing - Peace, Happiness
& Blessings-Dr. Janet Erickson, DD
http://www.janeterickson.com/spiritual-healing-blog/energy-healing/crown-chakra/232/#

3rd Dementia
Unconditional Love – no longer exists – by Mary the
Magdelen
http://www.2012.com.au/Unconditional_Love.html

The Third Dimension is Not Simple - by Venkat on July 11, 2007
http://www.ribbonfarm.com/2007/07/11/the-third-dimension-is-not-simple/

Emerald Tablet
Emerald Tablet – Definition
http://en.wikipedia.org/wiki/Emerald_Tablet

Issac Newton's Translation of the Emerald Tablet
http://www.alchemylab.com/isaac_newton.htm

Pineal
Pineal Gland – Definition
http://en.wikipedia.org/wiki/Pineal_gland

Pineal Gland – Our Third Eye: The Biggest Cover-Up In Human History – By Admin
http://www.wakingtimes.com/2012/06/19/pineal-gland-our-third-eye-the-biggest-cover-up-in-human-history/

The Pineal Gland and Melatonin
http://www.vivo.colostate.edu/hbooks/pathphys/endocrine/otherendo/pineal.html

85 Delete the 10% Blood Suckin – 85% & 10% according to Elijah Muhammad
Beliefs and theology of the Nation of Islam
http://en.wikipedia.org/wiki/Beliefs_and_theology_of_the_Nation_of_Islam

120 Lessons (Supreme Wisdom) by Elijah Muhammad (Lesson corrections by The Father Allah)
http://www.scribd.com/doc/58258079/120-Lessons-Supreme-Wisdom-by-Elijah-Muhammad-Lesson-corrections-by-The-Father-Allah

Devine Evil – D'Evil
Devil – Definition
http://en.wikipedia.org/wiki/Devil

Jay-Z Puts Illuminati And Devil Worshiping Talk To Rest On New Rick Ross Track "Free Mason"
http://hiphopwired.com/2010/07/10/jay-z-puts-illuminati-and-devil-worshiping-talk-to-rest-on-new-rick-ross-track-free-mason-audio/#KgUGLdcwa3Q8UC7e.99

7 Minus Sick

(Hip Hop Global Defacing)

7even Minus Sick

7even Minus Sick and Ignite were the first two songs on the God Damage Album that I wrote overseas while I was on tour with Public Enemy. At that time I had brought the band (The 7th Octave) on tour for the first time and I wrote 7even Minus Sick. I remember I wrote it in a hotel room skipping sound checks, skipping dinners, skipping all of that madness because I had to kind of get it out. It was about 7 being the God Degree and the sick shit that we as a people and individual with the God essence need to get rid of in order to be whole again. This gave me the idea of the 7 God Degree minus the sick shit and I called it 7even Minus Sick and I think if I can remember the hook it says "sick whit it and the shit that come whit it devil description of "God is forbidden" and what I was talking about all the sick shit that we kind of involve ourselves in that we are supposed to marvel at and when we are marveling at these things the whole psychology is we are to supposed to minus, snuff out the God consciousness. So the sick shit that we do I say in the chorus "God is forbidden" bigger than you to involve yourself in the sick shit that we do and have a God consciousness. If you had a God consciousness you wouldn't be doing the shit that you do, i.e. rappers being in these whack ass videos holding onto their Jesus piece or their crosses you understand what I'm saying swinging them back and forth. That verse laced with kind of metaphors and similes and meaning behind words.

7 Minus Sick

Written by: K. Shah pka Professor Griff

7even Minus Sick
The 7TH Octave
Title: God Damage
Label: Slam Jamz / Heirz To The Shah
Release Date: 2/1/2011

The state bomb the innocent
Fascist, wit this cashless ignorance
Sick shit, bent from the rotten stench
Of the governments sick fetish to kill the Un-Suspecting
Rex 84 King Alfred plan, Dead it
Heavy mental ghetto metal music

Ruthless tyrant divine evil the next clients
Still in the hood. I'm sill defiant
Anti I might be pre-pared for the anti Christ see
7 point 5 in the dome I be. Soci, Khari
School'em as to who I be........G. O . D.

A 60 child revolutionary wild style, I'm old skool
Break the dance, graffiti type krush groove
Who is the first, to utter the "N" Word
Dead dudes don't dance choose another verb

War is a racket by imperialist maggots
Buck fush and these demonic ass maggots
Melinated Godestry vs the devils trickkknology
Cast my pearls in the midst of swine PG.

HOOK 2X
Sick wit it, the shit that come wit it
Devil description, acts is forbidden
God description teach to uplift'em
Minus the devils degree cause GOD did it

"The same year they set up the IRS, they set up the FBI.
And the same year they set up the Anti-Defamation
League of B'nai B'rith...It could be a coincidence... [I
want] to see black intellectuals free...I want to see them
not controlled by members of the Jewish community."
* Louis Farrakhan speech quoted in the Dallas Observer
on August 10, 2000 Oklahoma City Bombing

----- The Honorable Louis Farrakhan

The state bomb the innocent

State-sponsored terrorism - terrorism practiced by a
government against its own people or in support of
international terrorism- the calculated use of violence (or
the threat of violence) against civilians in order to attain
goals that are political or religious or ideological in nature;
this is done through intimidation or coercion or instilling
fear.

Fascist, wit this cashless ignorance
fas·cism noun
1.(sometimes initial capital letter) a governmental system
led by a dictator having complete power, forcibly
suppressing opposition and criticism, regimenting all

industry, commerce, etc., and emphasizing an aggressive nationalism and often racism.

2.(sometimes initial capital letter) the philosophy, principles, or methods of fascism.

3.(initial capital letter) a fascist movement, especially the one established by Mussolini in Italy 1922–43.

Sick shit, bent from the rotten stench
Of the governments sick fetish to kill the Un-Suspecting

U.S. President Barack Obama personally signs off on all such "targeted killings," and while most are directed against foreigners – usually Muslims suspected of being radical jihadists – at least three Americans are among the hundreds killed in the last three years in drone strikes in Yemen, Pakistan, and Somalia. Hellfire missiles fired from unmanned Predators have become the president's preferred means of dealing "justice" overseas.

Rex 84 King Alfred plan, dead it

The same people responsible for the WTC disaster are the same people responsible for these camps. Destruction of the Trade Centers: Occult Symbolism Indicates Enemies Within Our Own Government. The world is being offered a "stark choice": join us, or "face the certain prospect of death and destruction."

Noam Chomsky Interview
The Gehlen Organization, copying Hitler's New Order, established a concentration camp system in San Luis Obispo County. It was called the California Specialized Training Institute. It developed plans called the *King

Alfred Plan, Operation Cable Splitter, Operation Garden Plot,* and *REX-84* and was later renamed as the Federal Emergency Management Agency (FEMA). You can get more information on these subjects from Militia of Montana, Bo Gritz, *Spotlight Newspaper,* etc.

There are over 600 prison camps in the United States, all fully operational and ready to receive prisoners. They are all staffed and even surrounded by full-time guards, but they are all empty. These camps are to be operated by FEMA (Federal Emergency Management Agency) should Martial Law need to be implemented in the United States. U.S. CONCENTRATION CAMPS: FEMA AND THE REX 84 PROGRAM

In a revealing admission the Director of Resource Management for the U.S. Army confirmed the validity of a memorandum relating to the establishment of a civilian inmate labor program under development by the Department of the Army. The document states, "Enclosed for your review and comment is the draft Army regulation on civilian inmate labor utilization" and the procedure to "establish civilian prison camps on installations." Cherith Chronicle, June 1997. CIVILIAN INTERNMENT CAMPS UP FOR REVIEW

Heavy mental ghetto metal music
Ruthless tyrant divine evil the next clients
Still in the hood. I'm sill defiant
Anti I might be pre-pared for the anti Christ see
7 point 5 in the dome I be. Soci, Khari
School'em as to who I be........G. O . D.

I am for the acquiring of knowledge or the accumulating of knowledge-as we now call it; education. First, my people must be taught the knowledge of self. Then and only then will they be able to understand others and that which surrounds them. Anyone who does not have knowledge of self is considered a victim of either amnesia or unconsciousness and is not very competent. The lack of knowledge of self is a prevailing condition among my people here in America. Gaining the knowledge of self makes us unite into a great unity. Knowledge of self makes you take on the great virtue of learning. Many people have attempted to belittle or degrade my followers by referring to them as unlettered or unschooled. They do this to imply that the believers in Islam are ignorant. If such a claim were so, then all the more credit should be given for our striving for self-elevation with so little. But truth represents itself and stands by itself. No followers, nor any other people are more zealous about the acquiring of knowledge than my followers.

-The Honorable Elijah Muhammad

A 60 child revolutionary wild style, I'm old skool
Break the dance, graffiti type krush groove
Who is the first, to utter the "N" Word
Dead dudes don't dance choose another verb

War is a racket by imperialist maggots
Buck fush and these demonic ass maggots

war on terrorism...............

Melinated Godestry vs the devils trickkknology

The following is from a letter Amir wrote to a correspondent who requested his views on Yakub and the making of the Devil.

Amir has written a small book entitled "The Symbolic History of Mr. Yakub" that he hopes to make available if he ever succeeds in retrieving it from a publisher.

I believe the History of Mr. Yakub to be wholly spiritual and symbolic, using physical White people to represent mental functions and states of mind. This is not unprecedented. The ancient Egyptian Kings were often depicted "smiting" foreign barbarians who were symbols of the wild passions in the Egyptian people, not actual physical conquests.

The Egyptian Kings "battles" were often against the "Asiatics". They symbolized people stuck at the Assiah plane of development, i.e., savages. The lower appetites were the actual Asiatics.

Master Fard and The Honorable Elijah Muhammad used the same approach. Fard called White people "cave men" and "cavey." It refers to underground (subconscious) influences that operate in the dark (ignorance). Yakub represents the left hemisphere of the brain and its related mental activities. He had "an 8 ounce brain" because the left brain corresponds to the 8th sphere of the Tree of Life. Yakub was a "big headed scientist," meaning he symbolized extreme left-brained arrogance, vanity and unrelenting pride. The Honorable Elijah Muhammad taught that the Black man has a 7 ½ ounce brain "while the White man has a 6 ounce brain." Well, put similarly sized people's brains on a scale and you'll see that brains weigh pretty much the same.

Cast my pearls in the midst of swine PG.

Once I picked up these two books, I learned why Muslims refrained from eating pork. For instance in Book II in the chapter titled "The Truth About Pork (The Pig)" the Hon. Elijah Muhammad writes:

The pig is a mass of worms. Each mouthful you eat is not a nutritious food but a mass of small worms the naked eye cannot detect. Worms thrive in the hog. When these worms are digested into your system, they cause a high birth rate to hundreds of new worms called larvae which travels the blood stream of your system and lodge in your muscles. These worms even enter your brain, lungs or your spinal fluid. They cause muscular aches, fever and many other symptoms of sickness. The worm has an amazing ability to go undetected in your system for many years. The scientific name for the ill-causing worm found in all pork is Trichinella spiralis which causes trichinosis.

Despite what veterinarians, public health officials, the Agricultural Department or your doctor say, the best defense against the pig is DO NOT EAT IT! When you do eat it, you do not hurt God, His Messenger, the Muslim or anyone else. You hurt yourself. Thorough and slow cooking of pork does not remove the danger of the worms found in all pork. Additional cooking of pork purchased in the summer or processed pork products does not make the worm-infested pork safe for eating. Inspection and governmental seals on pork do not remove the danger of the worms yet in the pork to make it safe for you to eat.

HOOK
Sick wit it, the shit that come wit it
Devil description, acts is forbidden
God description teach to uplift'em
Minus the devils degree cause GOD did it

Resource Information:

"It had adult classes which taught, among other things, mathematics, to help the poor Negroes quit being duped and deceived by the "tricknology" of "the blue-eyed devil white man.""
The Autobiography of Malcolm X

Melanin is important because it's the most primitive and universal pigment in living organisms. Melanin is produced in the pineal gland. Abundantly found in primitive organisms such as fungi, as well as advanced primates. Furthermore, within each living organism, melanin appears to be located in the major functional sites. For example, in vertebrates, melanin is not only present in the skin, eyes, ears, central nervous system, it can also be found in the pineal gland, pituitary gland, thyroid gland, thymus gland, adrenal gland, and the barathary gland. Melanin is abundantly present in the viscera, including the heart, liver, arteries, the muscles, and the gastrointestinal tract; thus, within each and every living organ which aids the human body melanin appears. Regardless of what color your skin appears to be all genes in all creatures on this planet are black because they are coated with melanin.
http://www.sankofa.ch/texts/Melanin.htm

War is just a racket. There are only two things we should fight for. One is the defense of our homes and the other is the Bill of Rights. War for any other reason is simply a racket. http://wanttoknow.info/warisaracket

The "War On Terror" Is A $6 Trillion Racket, Exceeding The Total Cost Of World War II and http://www.infowars.com/the-"war-on-terror"-is-a-6-trillion-racket-exceeding-the-total-cost-of-world-war-ii/

War Is A Racket Conducted
For The Benefit Of The Very Few
http://rense.com/general10/warw.htm

"The N word"
http://www.daveyd.com/nword.html

Let no one in any way deceive you, for {it will not come} unless the apostasy comes first, and the man of lawlessness is revealed, the son of destruction, who opposes and exalts himself above every so-called god or object of worship, so that he takes his seat in the temple of God, displaying himself as being God. Do you not remember that while I was still with you, I was telling you these things? And you know what restrains him now, so that in his time he may be revealed. For the mystery of lawlessness is already at work; only he who now restrains {will do so} until he is taken out of the way. And then that lawless one will be revealed whom the Lord will slay with the breath of His mouth and bring to an end by the appearance of His coming; {that is,} the one whose coming is in accord with the activity of Satan, with all power and signs and false wonders, and with all the deception of wickedness for those who perish, because they did not receive the love of the truth so as to be saved. And for this reason God will send upon them a deluding influence so that they might believe what is false, in order that they all may be judged who did not believe the truth, but took pleasure in wickedness.

(2 Thessalonians 2:3–12) —NASB

And there was war in heaven, Michael and his angels waging war with the dragon. And the dragon and his angels waged war, and they were not strong enough, and there was no longer a place found for them in heaven. And the great dragon was thrown down, the serpent of old who is called the devil and Satan, who deceives the whole world; he was thrown down to the earth, and his angels were thrown down with him.

(Revelation 12:7–9) —NASB

John Cox wrote:

OBAMA IS MABUS, THE ANTI-CHRIST, THE BEAST 666!!!

1.- He will come as a man of Peace (Obama promises peace in Iraq, defeat for the United States, a country he claims to serve.)

2.- He will come mounted on a white Female horse (Obama's mother is white who had 12 African husbands and lovers).

3.- He will come to deceive (Obama says he's a Christian but in fact he was born a Muslim, practices the Islamic religion and prays on Friday's facing Mecca).

4.- He will make himself the most powerful man on earth, if elected, Mabus will be his name.

5.- He will try to destroy the Jewish People and Israel (Obama has said he loves Arabs specially Palestinians, hates Israel and Jews. Admires Hitler, Osama etc.).

6.- He will present himself as good and righteous but in fact he's Satan himself violence and murder is in his heart.

7.- Obama will help Iran and Al Qaida in their evil projects.

8.- Barack Hussein Obama is the "King of the South" predicted in the Bible (Daniel .11, Kenya is south of Jerusalem).

9.- Obama comes to implant muslim Sharia Law upon America.

10.- Obama will enslave American women forever with Sharia Law.

11.-Mabus will finish his term on 2012, predicted to be the end of the world.

12.- Mabus will use Mind Control to obtain control of the ignorant masses, only those who read this note will be free from his mental hold.

13.-Mabus has come to destroy the finest country in the world, America. Mabus has come to steal your soul and your children's souls.

14.- It's written and will come to pass, Mabus will try to destroy the world with nuclear weapons but his first attack will be against Israel and the Jewish people. The beast 666 hates G-d's chosen people.

Obama is the Anti-Christ, beware of him and don't let you be deceived by him.

Supporters of Obama: 1.5 billion Muslims, Oprah, Louis Farrakanh, Jesse Jackson, Al Sharpton and all American Muslims. This time is your turn to suffer America, the next 4 years will be pure hell if Mabus becomes your King.

http://www.topix.com/forum/city/miami-
fl/TTM5S7RB6HF75RHNQ

King Alfred Plan/Rex 84

We are confident that the Minority would hold any city it took for only a few hours. The lack of weapons, facilities, logistics --- all put the Minority at a final disadvantage.

Since the Korean War, this department has shifted Minority members of the Armed Forces to areas where combat is most likely to occur, with the aim of eliminating, through combat, as many combat-trained military servicemen as possible. Today the ratio of Minority member combat deaths in Vietnam, where they are serving as "advisors," is twice as high as the Minority population ratio to the rest of America. Below is the timetable for King Alfred as tentatively suggested by the JCS who recommend that the operation be made over a period of eight hours:

1. Local police and Minority leaders in action to head off the Emergency.
2. Countdown to eight hours begins at the moment the President determines the Emergency to be:

    a. National

    b. Coordinated

    c. Of Long Duration (8th hour)

3. County police join local police (7th hour)
4. State police join county and local police (6th hour)
5. Federal marshals join state, county, and local forces (5th hour)
6. National guards federalized, held in readiness (4th hour)

7. Regular Armed Forces alerted, take up positions; Minority troops divided and detained, along with all white sympathizers, under guard (3rd hour)

8. All minority leaders, national and local detained (2nd hour)

9. President addresses Minority on radio-television, gives it one hour to end the Emergency (1st hour)

10. All units under regional commands into the Emergency (0 hour)

Overview of State-Sponsored Terrorism

http://www.state.gov/documents/organization/31944.pdf

Xfixciation

(The Story of the Gov't framing Hip Hop for the murder of Jazz, Gospel, Blues, Soul and R&B)

Xfixciation

There is a very Critical spelling:

It's the X which is the unknown, its the fix by the CIA, tion – Xfixciation. The concept of the song is simply about a story on how Hip Hop was framed by the United States Government and all the other genres of music was made to look like Hip Hop was the culprit. Hip Hop turned around and used all the other genres of music to prove that the Government is responsible.

So if you go into the chorus where it talks about jazz, the discos craze. You talk about songs that have us insane and want to blaze. These are the emotional responses to these particular genres of music simply because the culprit that was trying to destroy and call out all the other genres of music and blame it on Hip Hop was actually the United States Government. In a nutshell that's it. The story about conspiracy and Hip Hop conspiracy that Hip Hop was framed to take the heat as the United States Government murdered all the other genres of music.

Xfixciation
Written by: K. Shah pka Professor Griff

Xfixciation
The 7TH Octave
Title:God Damage
Label: Slam Jamz/Heirz To The Shah
Release Date: 2/1/2011

Verse 1
Here's the first thing,The 7- O must address
We want the culprits found, Suspects and mad arrest
Evidence, clues, witnesses, Ballistic shit
Keep in mind all this forensic shit it better fit
Several polygraphs, alibis and lab tests
Fingerprints, DNA, Yeah and those bulletproof vests
Not another cold case, We won't confession session
Cover ups, rap sheets, You better bet I'm checking
Not trying to make bail, I feel its all or nothing
Fuck interrogations, I think I'm on to something

Bridge
What about the cry of jazz, Got us past this critical time
What about the hold on soul that got us fucked up in the
mind
What about the funk, house, salsa and disco craze
What about the songs that's got us insane and wanna blaze
What about the blues, rhythm, yeah that lead to rock
What about the reggae tone, spoken word and hip hop

Chorus 2X
We the people we want justice now
Every tongue shall confess and every knee shall bow
Who, what, when, why, where, yo and how
Pop pop pop pop pop pop pop pop pow

Verse 2
I never had a record till I had a record go figure that
Never spit 16 till I spent 16 in jail and back
Never seen rappers doing shit behind closed doors
Never seen ladies go from house wives to house whores
Whats up with the dirty biz
Triflin treacherous, tricks and flicks
Framed by the peach fuzz
Lower chakras vibes and shit
Whats up with this clapping back
Whats up with this spitting facts
Whats up with this keeping real
Not when its comes to rapping black

What about this real talk
What about this real chalk
What about this white meat, pig swine and real pork
What about these elements
Gotta feel it, gotta love it
These candy rappers
They all come a dime a dozen
No body moving shit
No body buying it
Nobodys loving it

You can't deny the shit

Bridge
What about the cry of jazz, Got us past this critical time
What about the hold on soul that got us fucked up in the
mind
What about the funk, house, salsa and disco craze
What about the songs that's got us insane and wanna blaze
What about the blues, rhythm, yeah that lead to rock
What about the reggae tone, spoken word and hip hop

Chorus 2X
We the people we want justice now
Every tongue shall confess and every knee shall bow
Who, what, when, why, where, yo and how
Pop pop pop pop pop pop pop pop pow

Musical Vamp

Chorus
We the people we want justice now
Every tongue shall confess and every knee shall bow
Who, what, when, why, where, yo and how
Pop pop pop pop pop pop pop pop pow

The Hip hop community allegedly received this
anonymous letter on April 24, 2012 through e-mail. While
the person's identity can't be confirmed, and we can't know
for sure if it's true or not, the fact that we even consider

this to be another Willie Lynch letter tactic to destroy black people's culture.

---- Anonymous

Xfixciation is a work in and of itself. Trying to Alert the masses and music lovers of the dangers of corporate control of the music industry and its diabolical plan to fuze the genre's of music together to feed back to the masses a form "Soulless pop music" to sell products that only strengthens the machine world in its control of the "Mindless Sheepole" that they target.

I often thought about writing a song about this dynamic that is taking place in the "genre of all genre's" of music, Hip Hop. As I stand here on stage at the Soul Train Music Awards in Atlanta with *Raheem DeVaughn and Ludacris performing Bulletproof*, I was feeling that this song that kept coming into my spirit is a very necessary song, but I dismissed the idea thinking that this could only be done by artist such as *Slick Rick, KRS-ONE, Chuck D* or even *Ras Kass*. Then it hit me, I'm not sure if they see it from where I'm standing, I'm not sure if they understand it to the degree I understand it, at that point I began to plan to release the song. Having written some idea's down as I often do Xfixciation came to life, and writing with Khari Wynn we released the song on our second album The "GOD Damage".

Why, "Xfixciation" as opposed to Asphyxia or Asphyxiation (from Greek - "without" and sphyxis, "heartbeat") is a condition of severely deficient supply of oxygen to the body. This body that the definition speaks to is the body of music called "Hip Hop".

The spelling is apart of what I've grown to accept as our own form of communication in the hip hop culture, a form of ebonics. A way to have a conversation and lock other people out. Phraseology is important and the way it sounds more so than the way it's spelled is a very important aspect in the crafting of a rap song. Xfixciation means that the life force in hip hop was choked out of it on one level and on another "The Hidden Government" (ie) Illuminati which really runs this country and everything in it, framed Hip Hop and is responsible for the murder of the other genre's of music. Public Enemy's "Yo! Bum Rush the Show" Album, read across the cover "The Governement's Responsible".

Resource Information:

This story was written from a movie script I was writing about hip hop being framed for the death of all the genres of music.

Distractions

(We Interrupt This Message to Bring You the New World Order)

Distractions is the divided attention of an individual or group from the chosen object of attention onto the source of distraction. Distraction is caused by: the lack of ability to pay attention; lack of interest in the object of attention; or the great intensity, novelty or attractiveness of something other than the object of attention. Distractions come from both external sources, and internal sources.

Distractions

I wrote this sitting at a friend's kitchen table. The first thing I wrote was we interrupt this message to bring you the New World Order. As I sat at the kitchen table having to ink a song to record the next day it took me about 3 hours to do but none the less I felt it was very critical work because it wasn't hard to write because shit there is a whole lot of distractions. This particular song just pulling from what I experience every single day in just having a list in my head of what are the distractions, which as you know it's not very difficult right. Everyone could talk about the distractions that we have in our life but if you look at Webster's dictionary definition it talks about distractions as being divided attention of individual or group from the chosen objective or intention or of an intention unto a source that will distract you. I never really liked Webster because, Joel Noel whatever his damn name is, because they always use the word to describe the word. Diving into the lyrics, which will better help explain the song, I think the chorus will help explain some of those particular distractions. I said new consumer gadgets now you gotta have it, new trends are in for your fam and friends, non conscious actin baby bible packin black gods your lackin goddamn distractions. In dealing with one of the vamps which is the bridge to the song it speaks volumes because it says greek freaks is odd steppin in the yard meaning black people that have taken on and joined greek fraternities and sororities now steppin the yard worshipping white greek freaks. Face tats you hard of your enemies god, can you imagine black people getting the white jesus tattooed on their face. Non-conscious actin baby bible packin black gods your lackin goddamn distractions. That's Distractions in a nutshell. It don't take too much to deal with that you know in describing what this particular song is about and dealing with this synopsis.

Distractions
Written by: K. Shah pka Professor Griff

Verse 1
Broken fractions still acting like a helpless nig
Unidentified lies from a dirty pig
Preacher tripping still pimping it's the life you seek
Grass knowledge without the root
Yo the shit is weak
Confused at who you let come inside
No precautions so you lose, its due to fraternized
Nonfiction book bitching, You can't get enough
3- D claim you black, its not black enough

Chorus
New consumer gadgets, Now you gotta have it
New trends are in, For your fam and friends
Non conscious actin, Baby bible packing
Black gods your lacking, Goddamn distractions

Verse 2
Greek freaks is odd, Stepping in the yard
Face tats you hard, Of your enemies god
Non conscious actin, Baby bible pack'n
Black gods your lack'n, Goddamn distractions

On the net your chatting, About some non facts
Non public religious freaks, You coming back
But you can't understand, Why your $100 pants sag
Mom's through because she raised you in the Jesus bag

Knocked up can't abort loose and Running wild
Green dumpster in the back it claimed your third child
False pride ready to ride on some senseless crap
9 times out of 10 yea, that someone's black.

" ... 9-11 was a self inflicted wound ..."
------ Alex Jones

Broken fractions still acting like a helpless nig

Nigger (also spelled niggar): a word that is an alteration of the earlier neger, nigger derives from the French negre, from the Spanish and Portuguese negro, from the Latin niger (black). First recorded in 1587 (as negar), the word probably originated with the dialectal pronunciation of negro in northern England and Ireland.
      --*Anti-Bias Study Guide*, Anti-Defamation League, 1998

Unidentified lies from a dirty pig

"The Only Good Pig Is a Dead Pig": A Black Panther Paper Editor Explains a Political Cartoon
Mr. ASHBROOK. Is that really the case? I have in front of me a cartoon which shows, as you pointed out, a police officer depicted as a pig, and I suppose what they refer to as one of the brothers stabbing him in the back with all kinds of blood oozing out. And it says underneath it, "The only good pig, is a dead pig." There isn't any real way you could construe that into being a satire or being a commentary. That is about as definite as one could be. "The only good pig, is a dead pig," and here it is in the so-called Black Panther Coloring Book. How could that be

construed to be satire in the context of what you have just said, that it is all in the mind of a person? What possible connotation could there be in the mind of a beholder that would not be violence prone, murder prone or in a sense opening up a dialogue. That is what I gather from your statement, but it is not borne out by some phenomena.

Preacher tripping still pimping it's the life you seek

Theologians such as James Cone and others have begun to speak out against the teachings of many mega-church pastors because they tend to focus on worship as the path towards earning personal riches rather than as a tool to enrich the lives of people who grapple with injustice and oppression.
http://www.africanamerica.org/displayForumTopic/conte nt/128788938051211471

"As pastors, we have to link arms and have bi-partisanships. The [Black] church has always been the face of the community. Now we have to take on the responsibility of becoming true servants to the people from all walks of life. I get so mad when I see these pimpin' preachers driving Rolls-Royces, Bentleys, flying around in their private jets, and making it seem like prosperity and money is the way of God when 90 percent of your congregation is on Section 8 or can't figure out how they are going to keep their lights on or feed their kids. I'm big on perception, and what would it look like for me to live so lavishly if the people in my church are struggling?" says Pastor McClurkin in the article."

Grass knowledge without the root
Yo the shit is weak

grass·roots

1. the common or ordinary people, especially as contrasted with the leadership or elite of a political party, social organization, etc.; the rank and file.

2. the agricultural and rural areas of a country.

3. the people inhabiting these areas, especially as a political, social, or economic group.

4. the origin or basis of something; the basic or primary concept, rule, part, or the like.

Confused at who you let come inside
No precautions so you lose, its due to fraternized

Definition of "FRATRICIDE"
1: one that murders or kills his or her own brother or sister or an individual (as a countryman) having a relationship like that of a brother or sister
2: the act of a fratricide

Nonfiction book bitching, You can't get enough
3- D claim you black, its not black enough
Chorus
New consumer gadgets, Now you gotta have it
New trends are in, For your fam and friends

Non conscious actin, Baby bible packing
Black gods your lacking, Goddamn distractions

There is a question that is thought by many black people in the world, especially in America, but few ask the question and non dare call it a conspiracy. Does Jesus worship' hurt the black community? There is a new book that explains why and how this mystical fictitious character became real in the hearts of billions of people.

In an article written by Dr. Christopher C. Bell Jr. entitled the Black clergy's misguided worship leadership brings to the forefront the question most of all about but never asked by question Christians and non-Christians circles.

Here is an example of how reading, studying, researching and piecing apart writings such as this, brings about in depth in conversations that lead to actual lyrics that make up the songs. Whether you agree or disagree the body of information you're about to read serves as an interesting conversation piece.

Dr. Christopher C. Bell Jr.
"Jesus worship' is equivalent to 'white male worship' and is detrimental to the mental and emotional health of black people," argues Dr. Christopher C. Bell Jr. In this book, Dr. Bell cites cogent educational and behavioral reasons to explain why and how the glorification and worship of the ancient, Roman-made, white male, Christian idol, Jesus Christ is not only idolatrous, but how such worship subliminally makes black people complicit in their own psychological oppression. Specifically, Dr. Bell provides information to show that: Jesus Christ is the most influential figure on the planet, with more than 2 billion worshippers worldwide and many more who fondly study his teachings. But what if he never existed? Many skeptics have posed this very question, and while true believers scoff at such suggestions, the debate is far from resolved.

Jesus may have changed the world, but did he really walk the Earth? The Pharmacratic Inquisition DVD Part 4 of 12

The Negro a beast in the image of God. In placing this book entitled "The Negro a Beast" or "In the Image of God" upon the Ameri- can market, we do so knowing that there will be many learned men who will take issue with us, but while we are fully convinced of this, we are also convinced that when this book is read and its contents duly weighed and considered in an intelligent and prayerful manner, that it will be to the minds of the American people like unto the voice of God from the clouds appealing unto Paul on his way to Damascus. We have not brought out this book hurriedly and without due thought and consideration, but on the other hand we have had the manuscript under advisement for considerable time, and we have read and reread it until the ponderous, sledge hammer blows of Prof. Carroll rang in our ears until the clang and din of his arguments convinced us that it would be a sin before God and man to withhold from the reading public such an array of biblical, scientific and common sense arguments. We are placing this book before the reading public as a witness to be questioned and cross examined by the world, and if its pages will not stand the righteous attack of criticism, then we are willing for its arguments to be trailed in the dust of oblivion. We ask the reading public to carefully peruse its pages, and if in any particular there can be produced evidence that this is ok is not founded upon the bible *in toto*, and scientifically digested, then we are ready to close our doors, and place over its portals in burning letters of fire, "Deluded and Misguided by an Array of Biblical Truths Scientifically Discussed".

LIST OF ILLUSTRATIONS.

Is Adam and Eve the morning of the creation of man?

Is the White man in the image of God? If he is can the Negro be also?

Does "like beget like"? If so, could White parents beget a Negro child?

Was Christ a Negro? If so, God is a Negro as he is the father of Christ?

Was the first offspring of Adam and Eve a Negro, or was any of their children Negroes?

The Beast and the Virgin, or the Sin of the Century?

Did Nature blunder, or was God mistaken when he said "like begets like"?

Will your next child be a Negro? If the Negro sprung from Adam and Eve, then it may happen.

The Egg of Creation. Can you get a Duck from a Turkey egg* or a Dove from the egg of a Crow?

There were Natural results in the amalgamation of nature. "But there were false prophets also among the people, even as there shall be false teachers among you, who privily shall bring in damnable heresies, even denying the Lord that bought them, and bring upon themselves swift destruction." -2nd Peter 2:1

The "Jesus Christ" worshipped by black people is the ancient, Roman-made, white male, idol god created by Roman Emperor Constantine and church bishops of the Roman Church at the Nicene Council (CE 325), and hundreds of years later, white slave masters Christianized (or taught) their black slaves to worship this same white male idol god; whereas now the white male image of "Jesus Christ" is deeply ingrained in the psyche of both black and white people.

"The greatest miracle Christianity has achieved in America is that the black man in white Christian hands has not grown violent. It is a miracle that 22 million black people have not risen up against their oppressors – in which they would have been justified by all moral criteria, and even by the democratic tradition! It is a miracle that a nation of black people has so fervently continued to believe in a turn-the-other-cheek and heaven-for-you-after-you-die philosophy! It is a miracle that the American black people have remained a peaceful people, while catching all the centuries of hell that they have caught, here in white man's heaven! The miracle is that the white man's puppet Negro 'leaders', his preachers and the educated Negroes laden with degrees, and others who have been allowed to wax fat off their black poor brothers, have been able to

hold the black masses quiet until now."

— Malcolm X, The Autobiography of Malcolm X

The Jesus worshipping (white male worshipping) culture of the black community subliminally afflicts many black people with a deleterious white superiority syndrome (WSS) that leads to low self esteem, psychological dissonance, and emotional and spiritual depression resulting in self-limiting beliefs and aberrant behavior such as; low academic achievement motivation among black adolescents, mutual alienation between black men and women, increased feelings of hate toward whites and other blacks, and increased stress and other health related problems in black males;

"You have an historical Jesus, and the Honorable Elijah Muhammad told us 75 percent of what you read about Jesus and what he would do is a future man. It never was fulfilled 2,000 years ago," said Min. Farrakhan, addressing scholars of Christianity. "If Satan had two more thousand years to do his devilishment, the Jesus that comes on the scene at the end times, is the one to absolutely destroy the works of Satan. Jesus 2,000 years ago would be too soon, so he talked about one coming after him."

http://www.finalcall.com/artman/publish/National_News_2/article_8642.shtml

The Jesus worshipping (white male worshipping) customs of the black community reinforces, in both white and black people, the racist notion of white male superiority in the same ways as white racial discrimination and white racial aggression;

Question: "Is Christianity a white man's religion?"

Answer: In the past 2,000 years, the vast majority of Christians have been white/European. While Christianity had its beginnings in the Middle East, it spread rapidly to Europe and parts of Asia where Caucasians were the predominant race. The history of Christianity is filled with expansions, but mostly throughout Europe and Asia, then on to the West in the 15th century. Christianity has not had nearly the same success spreading among Middle Easterners, Africans, and Asians, and this has led many to declare that Christianity is a religion for white people.

The white male worshipping (Jesus worshipping) is so you who after years of embedment in such a culture feel alienated, demeaned, angry, and react in ways that lead to high rates of recalcitrance, self abuse, crime, violence, and incarceration.

Instructions to Laborers; ... An original man, ... W.D. Fard which contains 40 questions answered by Elijah Muhammad.

The following questions must be answered one hundred percent before submission of Student to said, Lesson No,1.

Who is the Original man?

The original man is the Asiatic Black man; the Maker; the Owner; the Cream of the planet Earth - God of the Universe.

http://www.supremewisdom.webs.com/lesson2.htm

The Jesus worship (white male worship) tradition within the black community is a black clergy-administered carryover from black peoples' past experiences as chattel slaves, and this tradition unwittingly ensures that black people continue to learn and believe, as their slave masters would insist, that "whiteness and the white male Christian power structure are anointed and approved by God"; a result that now leads to behavior and sentiments on the part of many black people that is reflective of a slave mentality and a "low caste group" self-image.

What does it mean when the Bible says that Adam was made "in the image" and "after the likeness" of God (Gen 1:26 King James Version)? And how does this relate, if at all, to the Nation of Islam Lesson (Student Enrollment No. 1) which states that the Original Black Man is "God of the Universe?" Few writers have discussed these two scriptural statements in the same context.

According to the Honorable Minister Louis Farrakhan, however, the two in fact make the same theological point about man. He says:

"Well the Bible tells you He (God) made man in His own image and after His own likeness. Well, He made you into a God."

"How could I be made in the image and likeness of God and not be God?"

The Jesus worshipping (white male worshipping) culture within the black community subliminally diminishes and demeans black manhood while buttressing, elevating, and glorifying white manhood; a result that stokes a latent anger, a temperament of violence, and self-injurious behavior in many young black men while promoting a sense of racial superiority in many white men.

The ritual process used by the ancient world to invite the spirit of a god to incarnate within its statue, a process called pit pi ("Opening-of-the-Mouth"), is similar to that described for Adam in Gen. 2:7: "then the Lord God formed man of dust from the ground, and breathed into his nostrils the breath of life; and man became a living being." Adam's creation as the image or tselem of God therefore means, not simply that Adam somehow "looked" like God, but that Adam was specifically created to be the very medium through which God had a presence on earth and through which He is worshipped. Simply put: Adam is God Himself in a material body on earth.

Dr. Wesley can be reached at drwesleymuhammad@gmail.com. His sources for this article include Andreas Schüle, "Made in the >Image of

God<: The Concepts of Divine Images in Gen 1-3," ZAW 117 (2005): 1-20; Hans Wildberger, "Das Abbild Gottes, Gen 1:26-30," ThZ 21 (1965): 481-501.

Dr. Bell argues that to neutralize the above negative effects of "Jesus worship," the black clergy must stop teaching black people to glorify and worship Jesus Christ and begin teaching them a "new Christianity" that espouses WORSHIPPING ONLY GOD the creator and sustainer of life and recognizes Jesus as a human being and prophet. Why? Because this "new Christianity" would promote Jesus Christ from the status of an unbelievable, make-believe, superstition-based, supernatural, extra-terrestrial god-character to the status of a believable, historically feasible, real life human being and prophet; and young black men will be able to relate to a "Prophet Jesus" and to his teachings with a sense of rationality, human commonality, and self-respect. None of these relationships is possible between today's Christianity and young black men.
http://www.drchrisbell.com/BlackClergyBook.html

True Islam's 1997 cult classic is back in print in a new, revised edition. The Book of God has been called 'the bible of the Black God,' as it presents a wide range of scientific, historical, and scriptural evidence demonstrating that the Original Black Man is the God of the world's religious traditions, from the religious traditions of the Ancient Near and Far East such as Kemet (Egypt) and India to the Biblical religions and Islam. The Book of God answers such questions as: How is the Black Man God and what does this mean? What is God's relationship to spirit and matter? What does Albert Einstein's mathematical revelation $E=mc2$ have to do with the Reality of God? If the Original Black Man is God, Who is the Original Black

Woman? Is there evidence of the reality of the Twenty Four Scientists? Who is Master Fard Muhammad? Was he actually an ex-con named Wallie Ford who served time in San Quentin on a drug charge? And more. The Book of God also demonstrates that: The God of the ancient religious traditions around the world was a self-created Black God. The Six Days of Creation in the book of Genesis chronicles the Black God's Six Trillion year evolution. The ancient sacred texts of the Original Man and Woman from around the world agree with the Hon. Elijah Muhammad's Teaching on God. The fields of Genetics and Hebrew Sacred Tradition converge to reveal that the Essence of the Creator inhabits the very genetic makeup of the Original Man and Woman. The Secret of the ancient Mysteries, the Masonic Lodge and Shrine, and the Church of Rome is the Reality of the Black God. Astrophysical evidence and ancient tradition converge to support the Hon. Elijah Muhammad's teaching on the Deportation of the Moon by a Black God.

Greek freaks is odd, Stepping in the yard

The establishment of the so-called "Black Greek Lettered" Fraternities and Sororities were imitations that modeled after Elitist Caucasian Greek Lettered societies in philosophical scope and organizational intent including adopting the cultural models of their counterparts. The majority of the "Black Greek" Lettered Societies were established after the 1896 infamous United States Supreme Court Decision of Plessy versus Ferguson, which ushered in Jim Crow Laws of segregation and institutionalize racism. These laws advocated the "separate but equal" doctrine and it allowed the practice of racial segregation and legal discrimination against African Americans in the United States. Blacks were prohibited and denied membership into white fraternities and sororities and this led to them establishing their own so-called "Black Greek" http://fahimknightsworld.blogspot.com/2008/11/black-greek-letter-fraternities-and.html

Face tats you hard, Of your enemies God

'Why Did You Put That There?': Gender, Materialism and Tattoo Consumption

ABSTRACT - Tattoos have traditionally been considered socially marginal and risky consumption choice in American/Western culture. However tattoos are now beginning to come into the mainstream of American life. They represent an interesting consumption behavior due to their permanent alteration of body parts and their relationship to personal expressions and identity. In particular prior research suggest important potential relationships between a consumer's tattoo choices and their Sex, Gender identity, Materialism, Uniqueness, need for Belongingness, and sense of Self-Control. Literature also stresses an important distinction between the Public and Private meanings that are associated with tattoos and the actual location and type of tattoo.

Joel Watson, University of Utah(1998),"'Why Did You Put That There?': Gender, Materialism and Tattoo Consumption", in Advances in Consumer Research Volume 25, eds. Joseph W. Alba & J. Wesley Hutchinson, Advances in Consumer Research Volume 25 : Association for Consumer Research, Pages: 453-460.

Non conscious actin, Baby bible pack'n

Black gods your lack'n, Goddamn distractions

On the net your chatting, About some non facts

Is the Internet a Blessing or a Curse?
Many people have mixed emotions about the Internet. For rock legend John Mellencamp, the Internet is seen in far more stark terms.

Reuters reported Mellencamp as saying during a public seminar at the Grammy Museum, "I think the Internet is the most dangerous thing invented since the atomic bomb... It's destroyed the music business. It's going to destroy the movie business."

Some may think Mellencamp's words are hyperbole coming from an artist looking for publicity. But in fact the Internet and the new technologies it has spawned have had a profound impact on our lives. As a result some things will never be the same.

Some institutions have suffered mightily at the hands of the Internet and online technology.
http://voices.yahoo.com/is-internet-blessing-curse-6849148.html?cat=15

Non prophet religious freaks, but you clappin back

Religions without prophets.
Sikhism: Formed in 15th Century AD as a reaction to the social and religious practices of the time in the Indian subcontinent. The Sikh Gurus (or teachers) have emphasized on recognizing all humans as equal before Waheguru (Guru Nanak), regardless of colour,

caste or lineage. The Sikh Gurus did not call themselves prophets. The emphasis is on a single all pervading God and creating a relationship with him. There is no place for intermediaries. The Sikh holy book is known as the Sri Guru Granth Sahib, Which was compiled by Arjan Dev Singh, added the teachings of 5 Gurus beginning with Guru Nanak Dev Ji and includes passages from both Hindu and Sufi saints. The Sikh Gurus have referred to their compositions as "dhur ki bani" or the word of primal divine source. Place of ritual is Gurudwara Sahib. Major locations of stronghold are States of West Punjab, NWFP in Pakistan & in India East Punjab, Delhi NCR, Uttrakhand, Uttar Pradesh, and Rajasthan. Major places of worship; Golden Temple Amritsar – India, Nanakana Sahib – Pakistan, Ponta Sahib – Punjab, Hem Kund, Nanak Matta – Uttrakhand, Gurudwara Bangla Sahib Delhi – India.

Buddhism: Founded by Prince Siddhartha Gautama of North India in 6th Century BC who was after his enlighten known as Gautama Buddha? Its sacred texts are Pali Canon (Tripitaka), numerous Mahayana sutras written originally in Pali. As per Tibetan Buddhism Monk is the spiritual leader. Buddhism follows the system taught by Buddha. Place of worship is Temple, meditation hall. Main sects in Buddhism are Theravada and Mahayana. Major locations of stronghold are India, China, Japan, Korea, Sri Lanka, South East Asia. Major locations: Sarnath, Gaya, Patna, Twang, Dharamshala, Leh, Laol Spiti, Gangtok – India, Colombo – Sri Lanka, Bangkok – Thailand, Cambodia, Guangzou, Lahsa – China, Bagan – Burma.

Jainism: Jains derive their name from the jinas, spiritual conquerors who have achieved liberation and perfection. Included among these are the 24 spiritual leaders called "ford-makers" or tirthankaras. The last of the *tirthankaras* was Mahavira (599-527 BC), a contemporary of the Buddha and the man generally considered the founder of Jainism. Jinas are believed to reside in the top level of heaven, above the realm of the gods. Accordingly, liberated souls are revered more than the gods. Formed in 550 BC, sacred scriptures are the teachings of Mahavira written originally in Sanskrit, major sects are Digambaras ("sky-clad"); Shvetambaras ("white-clad"), monks are the spiritual leader's place of worship is the temple. Major location is India. Major places of worship are: Palitana, Shankheshwar, Shikharji, Vataman, Mumbai, Mahudi Shri Ghantakarna Vir Temple and Ahmedabad – India.

Taoism: also known as Daoism was founded by Lao – Tze in China in 550 BC, based on the teachings of the Tao Te Ching, a short tract written in the 6th century BC in China. Its emphasis on spiritual harmony within the individual complements; Taoism is also increasingly influential in the West, especially in the fields of alternative medicine and martial arts like Tai Chi. There are two main strands and schools within Taoism, usually labeled "philosophical Taoism" *(Tao-chia)* and "religious Taoism" *(Tao-chaio)*. Tao Te Ching, Chuang-Tzu is sacred scripture originally written in traditional Chinese. Sage is a spiritual leader in Taoism. House of worship is temple. Major locations are; China, South East Asia.

Shintoism: Shinto (also Shintoism) is the term for the indigenous religious beliefs and practices of Japan. Shinto has no founder, no official sacred scriptures, and no fixed creeds, but it has preserved its main beliefs and rituals throughout the ages. The word Shinto, which comes from the Chinese *shin tao*, meaning "the way of *kami*", came into use in order to distinguish indigenous Japanese beliefs from Buddhism, which had been introduced into Japan in the 6th century AD. Shinto has no founder or founding date. When the Japanese people and Japanese culture became aware of themselves, Shinto was already there. Yayoi culture, which originated in the northern area of the island of Kyushu around the 3rd or 2nd century BC, is directly related to later Japanese culture and Shinto.

Among the primary Yayoi religious phenomena were agricultural rites and shamanism. Early shamans *(miko)* performed the ceremonies; eventually those of the Yamato tribe did so; on behalf of the other tribes and their chieftain assumed duties that led to headship of the Shinto state. Texts comprises of Kojiki (Records of Ancient Matters), Nihongi or Nihon shoki (Chronicles of Japan). Major location is Japan. Major places of worship are: Mt. Fuji, Dazaifu Tenmangu, Oyama Shrine, Toshogu Shrine, Tsurugaoka Hachimangu, Fushimi Inari Shrine, Ise Shrines, Izumo Shrine, Atsuta Shrine, Heian Shrine, Meiji Shrine all are in Japan.

Baha'ism: Also popularly known as Bahai Faith was founded in 1844 – 1882 in Iran by the two controversial leaders proclaimed to be the first preacher of Bahai named Bab & Baha ullah, declaring themselves as the prophets of modern world. The laws of the Bahá'í Faith primarily come from the Kitáb-i-Aqdas, written by Baha'u'llah, which is also a main scripture, it is sometimes also referred to as The Aqdas, "the Most Holy Book", "the Book of Laws" and occasionally the Book of Aqdas, originally written in Arabic and its title in Persian. The Manifestations of God are analogous to divine mirrors which reflect God's created attributes and thus reveal aspects of God without being incarnations of God's essence.

It is through these divine educators that humans can approach God, and through them God brings divine revelation and law. Bahá'ís believe that God expresses his will at all times and in many ways, and specifically through a series of divine messengers referred to as Manifestations of God or sometimes divine educators. The supreme seat is based in Israel. Major locations are Israel, Europe, US, India, South East Asia.

Greek Religion: Greek religion is the collection of beliefs and rituals practiced in ancient Greece in the form of both popular public religion and cult practices. Greek people recognized the major gods and goddesses: Zeus, Poseidon, Hades, Apollo, Artemis, Aphrodite, Ares, Dionysus, Hephaestus, Athena, Hermes, Demeter, Hestia and Hera though philosophies such as Stoicism and some forms of Platonism. Greeks believe in the afterlife or reincarnation. Their sacred texts are Hesiod's Theogony and Works and Days, Homer's Iliad and Odyssey and Pindar's Odes. Major Locations are Greece, Italy and Cyprus. Major places of worship were: Arcadia.

http://hatefsvoice.wordpress.com/2011/03/05/religions-without-prophets-list-of-those-religions-where-prophets-were-not-born/

Can't understand, Why your $100 pants sag

Sagging Pants: Prison Uniform Represents Wreckage of Black Communities?

The price tags on our youth's sagging jeans are nothing more than potential inmate numbers in disguise. Even more than the misappropriation of the word "nigga" as a term of endearment, the cultural phenomenon of sagging pants speaks exclusively to the institutionalized brainwashing of black America. If hip-hop is the voice of a generation, ass-sagging pants is the uniform, and both are rooted in a rebellion so entrenched that many black men proudly regurgitate, through words and attire, the tell-tale sign of psychological ownership. If we could delve beneath the often exploitative lyrics of poverty, violence, drug consumption and slangin', we might recognize that the price tags on our youth's sagging jeans are nothing more than potential inmate numbers in disguise.

"In prison you aren't allowed to wear belts to prevent self-hanging or the hanging of others," Judge Greg Mathis said in a 2007 interview for *Jet* magazine. "They take the belt and sometimes your pants hang down. ... Many cultures of the prison have overflowed into the community unfortunately," continued Mathis, who spent time in Detroit's Wayne County Jail as a youth. "Those who pulled their pants down the lowest and showed their behind a little more raw, that was an invitation. [The youth] don't know this part about it."

Homophobic – and unsubstantiated -- scare tactics aside, Judge Mathis' panoramic perspective as former gangbanger turned judge and prison advocate, suggests that the sagging trend is nothing more than a prison uniform encapsulating the wreckage of our communities. In urban war-zones of the late '80s and early '90s, as black men returned from lengthy crack-induced prison-bids, sagging pants were being worn on street corners simmering with freestyle cyphers and riddled with dirty needles. The beltless, low-riding style worn by "thugs" and "hustlers" became the symbolism of manhood, victimhood and the "hood" all in the same 16 bars.

http://www.alternet.org/story/156354/sagging_pants%3A
_prison_uniform_represents_wreckage_of_black

Mom's through because she raised you in the Jesus bag

Why? Because it is a psychologically thriller, raw and a profoundly honest appraisal of what it takes to survive in a racist culture in general, but in America's culture of racism in particular. "Only obliquely is "The Jesus Bag" about Jesus, or about religion, per se.

Only Psychiatrists with the heroic and patriotic courage to "see and tell what they see," can acknowledge that this festering sore exists at the base of American culture. It is hatred, sublimated hatred, disguised hatred, normalized banal hatred, and of course, the mother of all hatred -- self-hatred -- and the violence they spawn, as far as the eye can see. That is the unalloyed and unvarnished American culture as far as these Psychiatrists see it. Hatred, violence, sex and religion all pasted together under a veneer of pseudo-democratic normality is the crucible in which the witch's brew called American society is hatched. There it lies ever-simmering just beneath consciousness, waiting for the pressure to again reach the boiling point. The book details how in the vilest of possible moral acts, religion was consciously used to maintain control over black slaves, and later over black semi-slaves, and now over black "remembered slaves." The authors conclude that the experiment did not work, and that instead, blacks fashioned "their" religion into a life-sustaining force, which if continued on its present course, will be victorious and will overthrow the devils and drive them from the temple. But don't believe it.

The Jesus Bag William H. Grier

Knocked up can't abort loose and Running wild
Green dumpster in the back it claimed your third child

Michael Benjamin says: Among Non-Hispanic black teens, the abortion rate was even greater – 5,956 abortions to 2,265 live births, or 72%. For every 1,000 African-American babies born to teens, 2,630 were aborted. I wonder why black teens are resorting to abortion when contraception is so widely available. Given that this is the most sexually informed generation, I don't understand their actions.

This is an example of the untold stories of black women in these "Laboratories of death" Blacks need to know that "Abortions are not a form of birth control"
Day Gardner: "Yet Another Senseless Death As A Black Woman Dies Due To Planned Parenthood Abortionist"

The pro-life activist and conservative, in a statement: "Tonya Reaves, who was only 24, died Friday, July 20, 2012 on the operating table of a Chicago Planned Parenthood. According to a local CBS television station Tonya died of a hemorrhage due to an abortion. It is so heartbreaking and tragic that this young woman believed the continuous lies of Planned Parenthood who state that abortions are perfectly safe. The truth is that abortion is not safe for the women who experience physical and emotional problems for years and years after having an abortion -- abortion is not safe for the 4,500 innocent babies that are brutally slaughtered each and every day in America, and abortion is most certainly not safe for the young women who die at the hand of an abortionist."

Her statement continues about the situation: "Incredibly, Planned Parenthood was founded by a racist named Margaret Sanger who made it her life's work to limit the growth of the black population in America. She felt so strongly about this she initiated the 'Negro Project' in 1939. The objective of the 'project' was to infiltrate the black community by presenting birth control, sterilization and abortion as health options for black women. To this day, Planned Parenthood's billion dollars a year, genocidal formula continues to kill women and children -- with Black women and children being disproportionately targeted for abortion. This is no accident -- it's just business -- a very cruel and bloody business! I am so sad and angry about the death of this beautiful black girl and her baby. Tonya Reaves and her child should not have died!"

False pride ready to ride on some senseless crap
9 times out of 10 yea, that someone's black.

THE IDENTITY CRISIS OF THE BLACK ON BLACK CRIMINAL:

Negroes also have been not too subtly defined by the White majority in America as Public Enemy Number One in the so-called war against crime. To the extent this is true, their dominant contribution to our crime problem has been ensured. The conscious or unconscious tendency among middle class whites to equate Negroes with crime has given the latter a final shove into total degradation and alienation, providing a powerful nothing-to-lose incentive to criminal acts. EDWIN SCHUR Our Criminal Society.

FOR THE BLACK-ON-BLACK VIOLENT CRIMINAL, identification with the White supremacist aggressor community is never complete, nor is his dis-identification with the victimized African American community. The Black-on-Black criminal is a hybrid, a victimized aggressor one motivated and rationalized by his perceived victimization. Like all Africans subject to aggressive European domination he is neither Peter nor Paul. He is caught between the horns of an un-resolvable dilemma. He can never be a White man in the truest sense of the term, and he unalterably refuses to be a Black man in the true sense of the term. Having internalized the Eurocentric definition of what it means to be African all negative as well as having observed the material losses, social ostracism, victimization, rejection, etc., that Europeans and others have applied to those who identify themselves as African, he scurries to the safety of ethnic ambiguity or self- alienation. What in-between identity is chosen by the average African American, i.e., how much and what aspects of the White American racist aggressor and the Black victim he chooses to meld into his ambivalent personal identity, depends on many factors.

We must note that the Black-on-Black criminal as well as the average African American suffer most fundamentally from a chronically painful identity crisis from which they seek to find relief and/or escape. Many pathways to, and forms of relief are chosen, some more self-destructive and antisocial than others, all neurotic: many vacillating from one extreme to the other. Therefore, the average African American is synthetic, a Frankenstein creation of the American Dilemma. His synthetic identity is suffused with ambivalence, and based on misconceptions. For it is forged from two major falsified and self-serving Eurocentric projections a projectively inflated, confabulated, European image and a complementary deflated, scandalized, apparently and repulsively exposed African image. Consequently, the victimized African with no positive

African identity, and his identification with the false image of the European, can only achieve alienation from reality no matter how normal, law- abiding, abnormal, or criminal he may appear to be.

The Black-on-Black violent criminal, in forging his personality chooses to identify with, for whatever reasons, the violent, victimizing aspects of his White American racist aggressor, and attempts to reject or escape from his euro centrically falsified, victimized African American image. In so doing he paradoxically incarnates and fulfills the euro centrically projected stereotype of himself as criminal. His identification with his White supremacist aggressor is partial because he, on some subconscious level of his being, recognizes his own victimization by the aggressor, and seeks to revenge or compensate for it. He therefore aggressively or through subterfuge rejects the moral, ethical values and preachments of his White supremacist aggressors.

He recognizes they are designed not to be applied to their own behavior and attitudes toward him, but are designed to prevent his retaliation against them and to make his victimization and exploitation more efficient and trouble-free. The violent Black-on- Black criminal feels the common African American ambivalence more intensely than do non-criminal African Americans. He is most sensitive to it and therefore represses it more deeply. He disassociates or splits off the pain from the emotion and only feels the vague indefinable frustration, invisible restraining forces, the anger, the restlessness, agitation, irritation and moodiness; the boredom, sense of purposelessness and meaninglessness, the painful states of consciousness that cry out from alienation and for violent expression.

Thus, the violent Black-on-Black criminal in many instances, being neither Black nor White, is but an ambivalent empty shell of a man whose bottomlessness, vacuity, numbness, and lack of definition are the sources of his insatiable need to fashion an identity from current fads, eccentric dress and behavior. His voracious and rapacious greed, his need to consume conspicuously, to become a gluttonous devourer of things and people, reflects his ethnic hollowness. His need to intensify the painful feelings of others are emblematic of his need to feel something within himself, to have someone else know the pain he has so deeply buried within. He kills the other so as to share his own death of spirit, humanity and deadness with someone else. His need to define reality and himself outside the consensus of others reflects his unrealistic definition by others, and his attempts to define himself through violent intrusion into their reality.

The partial or complete fulfillment of these needs brings about in him an overpowering sense of excitement, aliveness, power, sensuality, imperial authority and masculinity (which he often equates with the capacity to injure and destroy others). Though he transcends the restricted world that surrounds him, he also experiences, simultaneously, an unconscious sense of guilt and self-condemnation. He cannot escape his ambivalence. Since his antisocial acts are the only ones which he assumes permit him to experience the overwhelmingly positive feelings just described (even his material acquisitions are only instrumental to evoking desirable feelings), and since his nympho maniacal emptiness rapidly consumes these feelings, his hunger too soon becomes more painfully insistent.

To repress his unconscious feelings of guilt, isolation, alienation and self-condemnation that threaten to break through to consciousness, he becomes helplessly addicted to those intoxicating feelings and the violent, antisocial means by which they are ameliorated. Even if he does not enjoy his use of violence, the Black-on-Black violent criminal sees it as instrumental to attaining the feelings to which he is addicted. As such, violence is at least secondarily positively reinforcing.

Black-On-Black Violence: The Psychodynamics of Black Self-Annihilation in Service of White Domination
http://www.blackpeopleparty.com/10.htm

Resource Information:

Tattoos & Permanent Makeup
http://www.fda.gov/Cosmetics/ProductandIngredientSafe ty/ProductInformation/ucm108530.htm

Internet: Blessing Or Curse
There are many reasons why the Internet is so controversial. The problem with the Internet today is the fact that anyone can access just about anything they want to from it. For example, pornography is a big issue because children are accessing adult content so easily without anyone having to know about it.

Also, there are some websites that allow you to watch people doing drugs. A lot of this stuff seems crazy and unbelievable, but it is true. There was a recent accident from a website like this. The website was allowing its viewers to get high over the Internet on webcams and cheer each other on. A 20 year old male died from a drug overdose in this situation.

The thing is right now cyber-space has no real laws that limit the actual access you have on the net. There are some laws that make it illegal and result in consequences, but they can only go so far. Another issue is that there is so much obscenity and violence that goes on inside online chat rooms, and the most frightening part about it is that it is so easy for someone to trick another person with their age and get you to meet up with them. This is very dangerous especially for children.

http://www.exampleessays.com/viewpaper/88915.html

'Sagging' Pants Law Unconstitutional

http://news.newamericamedia.org/news/view_article.html?article_id=d3a71d53ffb4b60ecbe6351c0ac0b1c0

The abortion rate among young black teens in America:

Abortion has been a touchy and personal subject for many years. Whether you are considering an abortion or just want to know more about the numbers of abortions, this article will provide teenage abortion statistics and information to help pregnant teens.

First of all there are about 1.38 billion women in the world who are in the childbearing years (ages 15-44). About 6 million women a year become pregnant. Many teenagers are also sexually active throughout the world. By age 20:

77 percent of women in developed countries have had sex,

83 percent of women in Sub-Sahara Africa have had sex, and

56 percent of women in Latin America and the Caribbean have had sex.

And a lot of unplanned pregnancies result. More than 25 percent of women in the world get an abortion. Compare this with the United States where nearly 40 percent of women who get pregnant have an abortion. Here are some more statistics concerning the United States:

About half of all pregnancies are unplanned

1.29 million abortions took place in 2002

More than 42 million abortions were carried out from 1973 to 2002

http://www.pregnantteenhelp.org/options/abortion-statistics/

2 out of every 100 women have an abortion each year. Many of these women have had abortions before. In looking at teens and young adults, more than 52 percent of abortions obtained are by women who are under 25. Around 66 percent of all abortions are obtained be single women. Teenagers obtain 19 percent of abortions. As of 2000, there were around 1800 places in the United States where a woman could get an abortion. Most abortions (88 percent) occur in the first 8 weeks of pregnancy. Teenagers are more likely to get a late abortion. .3 percent of all abortions cause hospitalization for the woman.

Beyond Trayvon
(White on Black Crime in Servitude of the Illuminazi)

On one of the darkest days of 2012 I had the pleasure of recording this verse with my two sons Rasheem (Ramega) and Khalil (Khalil Who?) at the studio in College Park, Georgia with my dude Trinity. As I read from my research, I ask them the questions I had asked myself...

What would happen if a black man armed with a handgun confronted "suspicious persons" in his neighborhood? What would happen if the "suspicious persons" were unarmed white teens, one of them was shot dead, and the shooter claimed self-defense?

This is not an exercise in mere speculation. We know what would happen in such a case. There would be no white mobs in the street chanting "No justice, no peace!" There would be no whites holding a "million hoodie march" in New York City. There would be no white equivalent of Al Sharpton, the professional race-baiter behind the 1987 Tawana Brawley hoax, leading marches in the streets of the shooter's hometown. There would be no Federal civil rights investigation by the Justice Department. There would be no comments from a president who seems congenitally unable to keep his mouth shut on matters involving left-wing political correctness. And there would be no national media attention from biased, left-wing "reporters".

White on black crime on servitude of the Illuminati which is borrowed from Amos Wilsons book "Black on Black Crime" or "Black on Black Violence" in servitude to white domination. Can I ask you a question? Sure. What would happen if a black man armed with a handgun confronted a suspicious white man in a neighborhood and shot him to death. He would have gotten beaten, hung, executed immediately. Exactly. So understand why I wrote Beyond Trayvon. Understand why there was a need for me being a father and grandfather alright. While there was a need for me being a black man myself and why I had to go back and pull from the depths of my being to write this one verse. Being on a song with other men like Chuck D, my son Khalil and my other son Rasheem all in the same song. In a spiritual way me and Chuck passing the baton back to that young generation coming up after us is very critical but we need to understand what is Beyond Trayvon. If we don't correct this situation with the Trayvon Martin case and him being murdered nothing is Beyond Trayvon. Your son being murdered and your two grandsons being murdered is Beyond Trayvon right or wrong. Right. We have to understand this particular dynamic Beyond Trayvon is nothing Beyond Trayvon until we correct this. So in the song I said from the pages of the Cress theory I know you hear me. If you're out there listen up, yeah I know you feel me. Do I as a grown man and do I look suspicious on this track with black in it with a black hoodie consciousness and black facts. Young kid was shot is the cry we heard like Emmit Till it was tears and it was heartfelt. No arrest warrants, no weapon found one eyewitness shared black body down. Then I said to myself I can hear it now it's the same old racist shit they are going to say he had a gun but it's the same old racist shit. Confessions of a trigger happy hit man, murderous homicidal nature is the racist plan burying our black boys of blood thirsty hunger games, face of racist white but they got no game. Stand your ground is a legalized lynch law and I said at the end of this particular verse you touch another black kid yeah you touch us all. So in writing this verse I felt the pain of all those black families who have lost family members due to the wholesale murder of black boys due to what Bobby E. Wright calls "Psychopathic Racist personality."

Beyond Trayvon
Written by: K. Shah pka Professor Griff

Beyond Trayvon
Public Enemy
Title: Most Of My Heroes Don't Appear On No Stamp
Label: Slam Jamz
Release Date: 6/2012

From the pages of the Cress theory, I know you hear me
If you out there, listen up, yea u might feel me
Do I look suspicious on this track, wit the black in it
Black hoodie, consciousness and black facts
Yo! A Young kid shot, is the cry we heard
Like Emmett Till, it was tears and it was heart felt
No arrest warrant and no weapon found
One eyewitness, black body down
I can hear it now, it's the same old racist shit
Thought he had a gun, is the same old racist shit
Confessions, of a trigger happy hit man
Murderous homicidal nature, there racist plan
Burying our black boys, Blood thirsty hunger games
The face of race is white, they got no shame
Stand your ground, Legalize lynch law
Touch another black kid, yea you have to touch us all

"If I had a son, he'd look like Trayvon," President Barack Obama" said simply at a March press conference at the White House. "I think [Trayvon's parents] are right to expect that all of us as Americans are going to take this with the seriousness it deserves, and we are going to get to the bottom of exactly what happened." He also said that Trayvon Martin's death makes him think about his own children and that he feels for the teen's parents. "I think every parent in America should be able to understand why it is absolutely imperative that we investigate every aspect of this, and that everybody pulls together—federal, state and local—to figure out exactly how this tragedy happened."

----- President Obama Imagines Son Like Trayvon

From the pages of the Cress theory, I know you hear me
(see the song Color Confrontation)
If you out there, listen up, u might feel me
Do I look suspicious on this track, wit the black in it
Black hoodie, consciousness and black facts

THE DEFINITION OF BLACK CONSCIOUSNESS
This is the paper produced for a SASO Leadership Training Course in December 1971 by Bantu Stephen Biko.

We have defined blacks as those who are by law or tradition politically, economically and socially discriminated against as a group in the South African society and identifying themselves as a unit in the struggle towards the realization of their aspirations.

This definition illustrates to us a number of things:
1. Being black is not a matter of pigmentation - being black is a reflection of a mental attitude.

Merely by describing yourself as black you have started on a road towards emancipation, you have committed yourself to fight against all forces that seek to use your blackness as a stamp that marks you out as a subservient being.

From the above observations therefore, we can see that the term black is not necessarily all-inclusive, i.e. the fact that we are all not white does not necessarily mean that we are all black. Non-whites do exist and will continue to exist for quite a long time. If one's aspiration is whiteness but his pigmentation makes attainment of this impossible, then that person is a non-white. Any man who calls a white man "baas", any man who serves in the police force or security branch is ipso facto a non-white. Black people - real black people - are those who can manage to hold their heads high in defiance rather than willingly surrender their souls to the white man.

Briefly defined therefore, Black Consciousness is in essence the realization by the black man of the need to rally together with his brothers around the cause of their oppression - the blackness of their skin - and to operate as a group in order to rid themselves of the shackles that bind them to perpetual servitude. It seeks to demonstrate the lie that black is an aberration from the "normal" which is white. It is a manifestation of a new realization that by seeking to run away from themselves and to emulate the white man, blacks are insulting the intelligence of whoever created them black. Black Consciousness, therefore takes cognizance of the deliberateness of God's plan in creating black people black. In terms of the Black Consciousness approach we recognize the existence of one major force in South Africa. This is White Racism. It is the one force against which all of us are pitted. It works with unnerving totality, featuring both on the offensive and in our defense. Its greatest ally to date has been the refusal by us to progressively lose ourselves in a world of colorlessness and amorphous common humanity, whites are deriving pleasure and security in entrenching white racism and further exploiting the minds and bodies of the unsuspecting black masses. Their agents are ever present amongst us, telling that it is immoral to withdraw into a cocoon, that dialogue is the answer to our problem and that it is unfortunate that there is white racism in some quarters but you must know that things are changing.

The importance of black solidarity to the various segments of the black community must not be understated. There have been in the past a lot of suggestions that there can be no viable unity amongst blacks because they hold each other in contempt. Coloureds despise Africans because they (the former), by their proximity to the Africans, may lose the chances of assimilation into the white world. Africans despise the Coloureds and Indians for a variety of reasons. Indians not only despise Africans but in many instances also exploit the Africans in job and shop situations. All these stereotype attitudes have led to mountainous inter-group suspicions amongst the blacks.

What we should at all times look at is the fact that:
1. We are all oppressed by the same system.
2. That we are oppressed to varying degrees is a deliberate design to stratify us not only socially but also in terms of the enemy's aspirations.
3. Therefore it is to be expected that in terms of the enemy's plan there must be this   suspicion and that if we are committed to the problem of emancipation to the same

degree it is part of our duty to bring to the black people the deliberateness of the   enemy's subjugation scheme.

That we should go on with our program, attracting to it only committed people and not just those eager to see an equitable distribution of groups amongst our ranks. This is a game common amongst liberals. The one criterion that must govern all our action is commitment.

Further implications of Black Consciousness are to do with correcting false images of ourselves in terms of culture, Education, Religion, Economics. The importance of this also must not be understated. There is always interplay between the history of people i.e. the past, their faith in themselves and hopes for their future. We are aware of the terrible role played by our education and religion in creating amongst us a false understanding of ourselves. We must therefore work out schemes not only to correct this, but further to be our own authorities rather than wait to be interpreted by others.

Whites can only see us from the outside and as such can never extract and analyze the ethos in the black community. In summary therefore one need only refer this house to the SASO Policy Manifesto which carries most of the salient points in the definition of the Black Consciousness. I wish to stress again the need for us to know very clearly what we mean by certain terms and what our understanding is when we talk of Black Consciousness.

Azanian People's Organization 2001.

http://www.azapo.org.za/links/bcc.htm

To Be African or Not to Be:

The ancestors, through Dr. Hilliard's genius, had directed African Psychologists to deal with "the real deal." Can we Be and not be African? While this level of question frightened many of us and made most of us uncomfortable, I think it is the only place for us, as African Psychologists, to begin. Accordingly, I would like to address the question of African American identity development from the framework of what is fundamental to our "Be" ing.

This question to be African or Not to Be becomes even more complex when one factors in the context of African people living in a non-African and/or anti-African society. Given such a context, I have suggested that the understanding of what it means to be African must be informed by what I have defined as the Triangular Law of Knowing, Being and Doing for Africans living in an anti-African reality. The three laws are (1) the law of (mis)knowing; (2) the law of (non)being; and (3) the law of (un)doing. These laws note that "if you don't understand White supremacy, then everything else you think you know will simply confuse you" - law of (mis)knowing; "If you don't exist according to your cultural essence (nature/spirit) then everything that you think you are will only be a diminishment" - law of (non)being; and "the experience of one generation becomes the history of the next generation and the history of several generations will become the tradition of the people - law of (un)doing. Several scholars (Carruthers, 1972; Nobles, 1978; Akbar, 1984; Banks, 1992) have suggested, the psychological understanding of African people, must be informed by the extent to which we understand the impact of white supremacy, the retentions, residuals, and radiance of the African nature/spirit and the reverberating power to reinvent ourselves.

In discussing the falsification of African Consciousness as it relates to Psychiatry and the politics of White Supremacy, Amos N. Wilson also noted specifically that, "In the context of a racist social system, psychological diagnosis, labeling and treatment of the behavior of politically oppressed persons are political acts performed to attain political ends. For oppression begins as a psychological fact and is in good part a psychological state. If oppression is to operate with maximum efficiency, it must become and remain a psychological condition achieving self-perpetuating motion by its own internal dynamics and by its own inertial momentum" Wilson, 1993: 3)". The Eurocentric mental health establishment, he rightly suggests, is a participant and beneficiary of the white domination of African peoples. Psychology and the mental health industry is a very important cog in the self-perpetuating machine of African dehumanization, mental disfunctioning, and dehumanization.

The discipline of Western Psychology's reason for being is, to a great extent, to nurture and sanction the imperialist and racist political regime which fathered it. In this regard, Wilson concludes that the explanatory systems and treatment approaches of Western Psychology ultimately must be exposed as "political ideology and oppressive political governance parading as empirically validated principles of psychological and medical science, and 'objective' psychotherapeutic and psychiatric practices" (Wilson, 1993:3). This is equally true with the act of theory development.

African peoples' psychology is fundamentally derived from the nature of the African spirit and determined by the African spirit's manifestation as a unique historical and cultural experience. This natural and instinctual psycho-behavioral imperative is coupled with a revolutionary drive to achieve physical, mental and spiritual liberation. Given this unique condition, Eurocentric Psychology and the mental health industrial establishment created by it as well as the African Psychologist who knowingly or unknowingly participates in it cannot provide adequate explanations, rationales, theories and therapeutic practices.

The position taken in this discussion is that what is needed is a theoretical and therapeutic practice that is centered in our own African essence and integrity. This position is in fact consistent with our raison d'être. The Association of African Psychologists was formed in part to utilize our skills to benefit the African community. Specifically the raison d'être of the Association was to address the significant social problems affecting the African community and to positively impact upon the mental health of the national African community through planning, programs, services, training and advocacy. It was clear then as it is now that the African community's mental health depended upon our ability to (1) resist and/or inoculate ourselves from the degradation and dehumanization resulting from the effects of White supremacy and (2) to advance and/or increase our human essence and vitalism resulting from the maintenance of our cultural integrity. What emerged from these two psychological imperatives is the ultimate recognition that if our practice, including theorizing, does not respect and reflect the African essence and integrity and if we do not exist and function personally and collectively according to our own treatment approaches of Western Psychology ultimately must be exposed as "political ideology and oppressive political governance parading as empirically validated principles of psychological and medical science, and 'objective' psychotherapeutic and psychiatric practices" (Wilson, 1993:3). This is equally true with the act of theory development.

African peoples' psychology is fundamentally derived from the nature of the African spirit and determined by the African spirit's manifestation as a unique historical and cultural experience. This natural and instinctual psycho-behavioral imperative is coupled with a revolutionary drive to achieve physical, mental and spiritual liberation. Given this unique condition, Eurocentric Psychology and the mental health industrial establishment created by it as well as the African Psychologist who knowingly or unknowingly participates in it cannot provide adequate explanations, rationales, theories and therapeutic practices.

The position taken in this discussion is that what is needed is a theoretical and therapeutic practice that is centered in our own African essence and integrity. This position is in fact consistent with our raison d'être. The Association of African Psychologists was formed in part to utilize our skills to benefit the African community. Specifically the raison d'être of the Association was to address the significant social problems affecting the African community and to positively impact upon the mental health of the national African community through planning, programs, services, training and advocacy. It was clear then as it is now that the African community's mental health depended upon our ability to (1) resist and/or inoculate ourselves from the degradation and dehumanization resulting from the effects of White supremacy and (2) to advance and/or increase our human essence and vitalism resulting from the maintenance of our cultural integrity. What emerged from these two psychological imperatives is the ultimate recognition that

if our practice, including theorizing, does not respect and reflect the African essence and integrity and if we do not exist and function personally and collectively according to our own African essence (nature), then everything we do or provide (teaching, service, treatment and theorizing) will only dis-serve and de-humanize ourselves and our people.
http://www.iasbflc.org/old/Articles/Afrikanornot/afrikano rnot03.htm

Young kid shot, is the cry we heard
Like Emmitt Til, it was tears and it was heart felt

Emmett Till (1941-1955) was a black 14-year-old from Chicago who was brutally mutilated and killed in the Deep South in August 1955. The young man was visiting relatives in Mississippi when he allegedly whistled at a white female store clerk. Till was sharing a bed with his 12-year-old cousin when two white men came to get him on the morning of August 28; he was not seen alive again. His body was later found in a river, tied to a cotton-gin fan with barbed wire. An all-white jury acquitted the store clerk's husband, Roy Bryant, and half-brother, J. W. Milman, of the crime. The events stirred anger in the black community and among civil rights proponents in general, setting off the civil rights movement.

For four decades, Till's grisly murder continued to deeply trouble many, who believed justice could still be served. Though no one was ever convicted of the crime, and the two men who were tried for it had, by 2005, died, some of Till's family and friends, as well as investigators, believed others who participated in the lynching might still be alive. In a quest for clues, Till's body was disinterred in June

2005 to gather evidence. He was reburied in a quiet funeral. The Till family hoped the pending investigation would yield answers and justice.
http://www.answers.com/topic/who-was-emmett-till#ixzz27stLi1Gv

No arrest warrant and no weapon found
One eye witness, black body down
I can hear it now, it's the same old racist shit
Thought he had a gun, is the same old racist shit

Merriam-Webster's online dictionary defines "racism" as:
A belief that race is the primary determinant of human traits and capacities and that racial differences produce an inherent superiority of a particular race. Another definition in common usage: "Racism is power plus prejudice." Therefore, powerless minorities can never be racist, no matter how much they hate you for your melanin deficiency.

Please share this article by using the link below. When you cut and paste an article, Taki's Magazine misses out on traffic, and our writers don't get paid for their work.
http://takimag.com/article/what_is_a_racist_steve_brown e/print#ixzz27suwx6bo

Confessions , of a trigger happy hit man
Murderous homicidal nature, there racist plan
Burying our black boys, Blood thirsty hunger games
The face of race is white, they got no shame

Most of us don't know – in many respects, we already live in Panem, the authoritarian high-tech dictatorship described in The Hunger Games. The film shows us what we have to look forward to if we don't turn things around.

Its interesting The Hunger Games author Suzanne Collins gave her dystopian nation an appropriate name – Panem, from the Latin phrase "Panem et Circenses" which means "Bread and Circuses." It was the basic Roman recipe for the required amusement and distraction of the masses existing within a military dictatorship.
www.infowars.com/deep-secrets-of-the-hunger-games-exposed/

Stand your ground, Legalize lynch law

Zimmerman judge denied 'stand your ground' claim in earlier case. Her decision offers clues on what the defendant may face if he presses his self-defense claim in the killing of an unarmed teen in Florida.

George Zimmerman, shown in a sheriff's booking photo, is charged with second-degree murder in the shooting death of Trayvon Martin, an unarmed African American teenager, in Sanford, Fla., on Feb. 26. (Seminole County Sheriff's Office / June 3, 2012)

Many killers who go free with Florida 'stand your ground' law have history of *violence*. A Tampa Bay Times analysis of stand your ground cases found that it has been people like Moorer — those with records of crime and violence — who have benefited most from the controversial legislation. A review of arrest records for those involved in more than 100 fatal stand your ground cases shows:

• Nearly 60 percent of those who claimed self-defense had been arrested at least once before the day they killed someone.

• More than 30 of those defendants, about one in three, had been accused of violent crimes, including assault, battery or robbery. Dozens had drug offenses on their records.

• Killers have invoked stand your ground even after repeated run-ins with the law. Forty percent had three arrests or more. Dozens had at least four arrests.

• More than a third of the defendants had previously been in trouble for threatening someone with a gun or illegally carrying a weapon.

• In dozens of cases, both the defendant and the victim had criminal records, sometimes related to long-running feuds or criminal enterprises. Of the victims that could be identified in state records, 64 percent had at least one arrest. Several had 20 or more arrests.

Florida's stand your ground law has been under intense scrutiny since George Zimmerman claimed self-defense after killing 17-year-old Trayvon Martin at a Sanford apartment complex Feb. 26. Police and prosecutors said they did not immediately charge Zimmerman because they could not disprove his self-defense claim.

All told, 119 people are known to have killed someone and invoked stand your ground. Those people have been arrested 327 times in incidents involving violence, property crimes, drugs, weapons or probation violations. That does not include more than 100 traffic violations and other minor arrests not considered in the analysis.

The Times' background checks relied on Florida Department of Law Enforcement records, which log arrests within the state. The records do not always show when arrests end in conviction, and it is likely that many did not.

And of course, having an arrest record doesn't mean you give up your right to defend yourself in the future. A person who was guilty of something in the past may be utterly innocent in a different case now.

In some cases examined by the Times, a defendant's prior arrests occurred years before their fatal confrontation and therefore may reveal nothing about their propensity for trouble. For example, Max Wesley Horn Jr. successfully claimed self-defense after he shot a man during a 2010 dispute in New Port Richey. The arrests on Horn's record — for battery, larceny and for violating probation — were more than 15 years old.

"The legislators wrote this law envisioning honest assertions of self-defense, not an immunity being seized mostly by former criminal defendants trying to lie their way out of a murder," said Kendall Coffey, a former U.S. attorney from South Florida.

Coffey said the most troubling part about habitual offenders using the law is that their experience may have taught them how to manipulate the system.

"People who've been through the legal system are going to be more seasoned to using the law to their advantage," Coffey said. "And it doesn't take a master of fiction to write in a few lines of the script to turn a homicide into a stand your ground case."

Repeated arrests
When detectives investigate a homicide, they check the arrest record of their suspect as a matter of course.

Having a record can impact how defendants are treated, including how hefty a sentence they face and even how believable they are to police and prosecutors. Stand your ground cases are no different.

The Times analysis found that 67 percent of all defendants who invoked the law went free. For defendants who had at least one arrest, the success rate dropped to 59 percent. Serial law-breakers — those with three or more arrests — walked free only 45 percent of the time.

Even so, killers with repeated run-ins with the law and with violent accusations in their past have successfully claimed stand your ground across the state.

http://www.tampabay.com/news/courts/criminal/many-killers-who-go-free-with-florida-stand-your-ground-law-have-history/1241378

Touch another black kid you have to touch us all

Brake The Law
Written by: K. Shah pka Professor Griff

Confrontation Camp
Title: Objects In The Mirror Are Closer Than They Appear
Label: Artemis Records
Release Date: 8/8/2000

I had a dream that one day That the boys in black and blue
Won't understand you
Now raise your right hand, and Repeat after me
See, how do you shoot a cop
You grab the video cam pop in the tape, and commence to
pop
Something like the Rodney King shit
Caught a case and some lead And fed with the bullshit
You ain't got no rights
You gave the power to the one you ready to fight
You the average citizen
Your citizen shit ain't said shit and its news to them
So here I am come n Frisk me
So here I stand, Come and get me
See if I give a fuck, Spit bitch and see if I even duck
I made it through the harbour and can't even trust the law
Put the brakes on....."whore"
Objects in the mirror are closer than they appear

Resource Information:

Black on Black violence in servitude of white domination
Amos Wilson
BlackHeritageStamps.com
http://blackheritagestamps.com/search-welcome.html

Fourteen-year-old Emmett Till was visiting relatives in
Money, Mississippi on August 24, 1955 when he
reportedly flirted with a white cashier at a grocery store.
Four days later, two white men kidnapped Till, beat him,
and shot him in the head. The men were tried for murder,
but an all-white, male jury acquitted them. Till's murder
and open casket funeral galvanized the emerging civil
rights movement.
http://www.biography.com/people/emmett-till-507515

Killer-Cops and the War on Black America
http://blackagendareport.com/content/killer-cops-and-
war-black-america

Black cop shot 28 times by white cops - and accused of
murder
http://rt.com/usa/news/shot-white-murder-morgan-263/

Report: States With Stand Your Ground Laws See More
Homicides
http://thinkprogress.org/justice/2013/01/03/1390221/repo
rt-states-with-stand-your-ground-laws-see-more-
homicides/?mobile=nc

USLegal » Legal Definitions Home » Lynching Law &
Legal Definition

A lynching is a killing by a mob of people. In efforts to lobby Congress to enact a law against lynchings, in 1921 the NAACP proposed setting the size of the mob at no fewer than five. The NAACP later agreed that for a killing to qualify as a lynching, the killers had to act under pretext of service to justice, their race or tradition. Lynchings were more common in the post-Reconstruction South, where southern whites used lynching and other terror tactics to intimidate blacks into political, social, and economic submission.
http://definitions.uslegal.com/l/lynching/

Jim Crow (jĭm' krō')
The systematic practice of discriminating against and segregating Black people, especially as practiced in the American South from the end of Reconstruction to the mid-20th century. Upholding or practicing discrimination against and segregation of Black people: Jim Crow laws; a Jim Crow town. Reserved or set aside for a racial or ethnic group that is to be discriminated against: "I told them I wouldn't take a Jim Crow job" (Ralph Bunche).
Readmore:http://www.answers.com/topic/jim-crow#ixzz2Hsu8ha36

A Long History of Affirmative Action - For Whites many middle-class white people, especially those of us from the suburbs, like to think that we got to where we are today by virtue of our merit - hard work, intelligence, pluck, and maybe a little luck. And while we may be sympathetic to the plight of others, we close down when we hear the words "affirmative action" or "racial preferences." We worked hard, we made it on our own, the thinking goes, why don't 'they'? After all, the Civil Rights Act was enacted almost 40 years ago. What we don't readily acknowledge is that racial preferences have a long, institutional history in this country - a white history. Here are a few ways in which government programs and practices have channeled wealth and opportunities to white people at the expense of others.

http://academic.udayton.edu/race/04needs/affirm22.htm

ICE BREAKER
(Immigration Issue in Amerikkka)

The messenger asked the question, how can we free ourselves using the enemies language? I often pondered that question, failing ninth grade Spanish class and not knowing the different cultural dialects how would I ever understand the revolution from our brown brothers and sisters perspective? How could I ever begin to find the common ground to unite our cause to fight the same enemy. Watching channel zero one day I was dazed by the conversation that was taking place. The talking heads on the"boob tube". Acting as a modern day lynch mob were talking about who is illegal and who is alien in America? This particular conversation led me to think about the plight of the Native Americans in this country. As I began to study history to develop this song importantly to a time where Mexicans and Native Americans owned the vast majority of land in America. Aliens and foreign troops were considered European. As whites in America began to claim land that belonged to the natives laws were enacted land rights were enacted in the genocide began. The question in 2013 is all the real citizens of America or better yet while the real citizens of the United States of America. This song was written to bring attention to the plight of the original land owners in America. This song was written and recorded so that the original landowners would have a voice to the medium of hip-hop hopefully the attention that this song will get may bring some degree of understanding to all the homegrown terrorists what is state-sponsored terrorism of the real Steelers of the land in America what are borderless borders or rights to the land in America for the foreign troops on foreign soil is there a connection between undocumented workers in Nazi Germany and what is ICE? This is a government agency that has the right to arrest, detain, jail and execute the original landowners in America. (ICE) stands for the U.S. Immigration and Customs Enforcement.

ICE BREAKER
Written by: K. Shah pka Professor Griff

Ice Breaker
Public Enemy
Title: Most Of My Heroes Don't Appear On No Stamp
Label: Slam Jamz
Release Date: 6/2012

Home grown terrorist, for the benefit
Can't find a title or a name that truly fits
These land jackers, pale face land grabbers
Caught in a border war, the stench from the border whore
Real demons, feinin for a real reason
Can't truss em cause they always fuckin schemin
Broke treaty's wit the redman, dam
Klan disqized as fam, fuck uncle sam
Pause for the cause, open the mental doors
Foreign invaders, human traffic traders
Un-documented workers, want it back
Panic when the Brown man link wit the pro blacks
Who's the real citizen, have you ever been
You raped and robbed every people that ever let you in
Legalized theft, of the natives land
Speak with a fork tongue, rum and gun in hand

Chorus
The I C E,
Who get's the deported and who goes free
Who get's detained and remains

Who get's a card and who get's the blame

"This war did not spring up on our land, this war was brought upon us by the children of the Great Father who came to take our land without a price, and who, in our land, do a great many evil things..This war has come from robbery - from the stealing of our land."

"http://www.legendsofamerica.com/na-spottedtail.html"

Spotted Tail

Home grown terrorist, for the benefit
Can't find a title or a name that truly fits

The most dangerous enemy is the one who most resembles you. That is why the danger of white supremacy is so underestimated as a severe domestic terror threat. White supremacy is the true "homegrown" terrorism, dating back to the 18th century in the United States. White supremacy is the greatest danger we as Americans face as a source of domestic terrorism, and one of the least recognized. It is difficult for law enforcement, as well as ordinary white Americans, to recognize the extraordinary threat coming from those who look like them in terms of race. That makes them all the more dangerous.

http://www.washingtonpost.com/blogs/guest-voices/post/white-supremacy-the-real-homegrown-terrorism/2012/08/07/1603addc-e0e3-11e1-8fc5-a7dcf1fc161d_blog.html

These land jackers, pale face land grabbers

Caught in a border war, the stench from the border whore
Real demons, feinin for a real reason
Can't truss em cause they always fuckin schemin.

Editor's Note: To many Native Americans, Thanksgiving is a "Day of Mourning" that marks the genocide of thousands of Native Americans, the theft of Native lands and the assault on Native cultures. A few hundred Native Americans plan to gather along Plymouth shore to tell the stories of their ancestors. Viji Sundaram is the health editor for New America Media.

Today, while the aroma of stuffed turkey, apple pie, mashed potatoes and cranberry sauce fills kitchens across the United States, a few hundred people will gather along the shores of Plymouth and observe what they call their "National Day of Mourning."
http://news.newamericamedia.org/news/view_article.html ?article_id=56ca063b8d1a504cc6fcea979f74b993

Broke treaty's wit the redman, dam
Klan disqized as fam, fuck uncle sam
Pause for the cause, open the mental doors
Foreign invaders, human traffic traders

THE TRAIL OF BROKEN TREATIES

We need not give another recitation of past complaints nor engage in redundant dialogue of discontent. Our conditions and their cause for being should perhaps be best known by those who have written the record of America's action against Indian people. In 1832, Black Hawk correctly observed: You know the cause of our making war. It is known to all white men. They ought to be ashamed of it.

The government of the United States knows the reasons for our going to its capital city. Unfortunately, they don't know how to greet us. We go because America has been only too ready to express shame, and suffer none from the expression - while remaining wholly unwilling to change to allow life for Indian people.

We seek a new American majority - a majority that is not content merely to confirm itself by superiority in numbers, but which by conscience is committed toward prevailing upon the public will in ceasing wrongs and in doing right. For our part, in words and deeds of coming days, we propose to produce a rational, reasoned manifesto for construction of an Indian future in America. If America has maintained faith with its original spirit, or may recognize it now, we should not be denied. Press Statement issued: October 31, 1972.

TRAIL OF BROKEN TREATIES 20-POINT POSITION PAPER
http://www.aimovement.org/ggc/trailofbrokentreaties.html

Un-documented worker, want it back
Panic when the Brown man link wit the pro blacks

Illegal immigration and undocumented workers in America
The topic of illegal immigrant workers has recently become a high-profile topic in American politics and news. Characterizing this issue as having only two sides

may not give a full picture of the situation. This is a very complex topic that spans several areas. People from around the world today that wish to visit America for work, studies and/or travel might become confused by the diverse news stories currently being published.

First, one should realize that 2006 is an election year in the United States. Many politicians will try to use immigration and foreign workers as issues for their publicity campaigns. People from all sides of these issues will present data and personal interpretations in ways that they feel will provide opportunities for election or re-election of politicians favorable to a particular viewpoint. Sometimes this "news" is little more than an opinion and may well cross the line into overt propaganda.

It is perceived by some in the US that foreign workers are taking jobs that Americans should have, creating hardship for Americans that are finding difficulty finding jobs. Also, it is felt that people illegally in the country create a burden upon legal residents and citizens who pay substantial taxes. Undocumented residents do not pay taxes for government services, yet many receive these services while tax-paying citizens sometimes cannot qualify. At the same time many Americans would say that the US as a nation of immigrants depends on immigration for its continued success as an economic superpower.

It is estimated that approximately 12 million people are illegally residing and working in the United States. Many of them are Mexicans. Due to such a large number, Mexicans have become highly visible in recent news, and thus are the focus of many discussions. Further, people of Mexican heritage take pride in their origins and celebrate their culture and language, something that enhances the visibility of such a large population.

http://www.workpermit.com/news/us/2006_05_05/illegal
_immigration_and_undocumented_workers.htm

Who's the real citizen, have you ever been
You raped and robbed every people that ever let you in

The terms "black" or "Black" and "African American" are both frequently used to refer to Americans with African ancestry. There is some confusion over which term is appropriate, which can be distressing to people who wish to avoid causing offense, and the matter is further complicated by divisions within the community of Americans of African ancestry about which term to use. If possible, the best way to answer the question of which term to use is to ask the person to whom you are referring about his or her term of preference.

It is much easier to outline the terms which are no longer considered appropriate; *colored* and *negro*, for example, are generally considered offensive by Americans of African ancestry. Although organizations like the National Association for the Advancement of Colored People (NAACP) and the United Negro College Fund use these outdated terms, the inclusion of these offensive terms reflects the age of the organization, not permission to use outdated racial slang. These organizations have struggled over their names, ultimately deciding to keep the outdated terminology for name recognition purposes. "Mulatto" or "mulatta" in reference to a biracial individual is also offensive.

Use of the term "black" dates to the 1960s and 1970s and the civil rights movement. The Black Power movement advocated strongly for the use of "black" to replace the outdated "negro," and many Americans of African ancestry started to embrace the term. Others preferred "Afro American," an early blending of "African" and "American." In the 1980s, "African American" began to see common usage, and the term quickly became very popular.

The argument for saying "black" is that it is a term which refers purely to skin color, recognizing the fact that people from Africa come in a variety of shades and hues. Using "black" also allows people to distinguish between Americans with slave ancestors, who may not have a close connection with Africa, and recent immigrants from Africa. This term also includes Americans of slave ancestry who immigrated from the Caribbean, as these individuals may feel more closely connected to places like Haiti or Jamaica than Africa.

People may also prefer to use "black" because it encompasses people who are biracial, allowing people who self-identify as black to use the term, even if their ancestry is mixed. Others use the term as a matter of pride, celebrating their skin color and their cultural identity. The term also allows users to connect with other people with similar heritage all over the world, much like "white" connects people with light skin, and "brown" connects people with a variety of skin tones.

In favor of "African American" is the long-established custom in the United States of referring to people with ethnic ancestry as "Ethnicity American," as in "Japanese American," "German American," or "Greek American." The term is meant to recognize the African ancestry of all Americans with African heritage, whether they immigrated from Ghana last week or are descended from slaves brought to America in the 1500s. Some people prefer this usage because it includes a nod of respect to their ethnic heritage.

If you aren't sure about which term is appropriate, it is probably safest to use "African American," because most people understand that people are trying to be respectful when they use this term. You may be gently corrected by someone who prefers to be referred to as "black," but he or she will usually understand that your intentions in saying "African American" were good.

http://www.wisegeek.com/should-i-say-black-or-african-american.htm

Legalized theft, of the natives land
Speak with a fork tongue, rum and gun in hand
Chorus
The I C E,
Who get's the deported and who goes free
Who get's detained and remains
Who get's a card and who get's the blame

http://gulagamerika.homestead.com
http://rense.com/general17/statebystate.htm
http://rense.com/general67/femm.htm
Who is a Green Card Holder (Permanent Resident)?

A Green Card holder (permanent resident) is someone who has been granted authorization to live and work in the United States on a permanent basis. As proof of that status, a person is granted a permanent resident card, commonly called a "Green Card." You can become a permanent resident several different ways. Most individuals are sponsored by a family member or employer in the United States. Other individuals may become permanent residents through refugee or asylee status or other humanitarian programs. In some cases, you may be eligible to file for yourself.

This page can be found at: http://www.uscis.gov/greencard

Resource Information:

Operation Gladio was AMERICAN State-Sponsored TERRORISM in Europe
http://fromthetrenchesworldreport.com/operation-gladio-was-american-state-sponsored-terrorism-in-europe/29053/

American State Terrorism
A Critical Review of The Objectives of U.S. Foreign Policy in The Post-World War II Period
http://www.mediamonitors.net/mosaddeq13.html

Arizona Immigration Law Costing The State Millions Every Year: Report
http://www.huffingtonpost.com/2013/01/02/arizona-immigration-law_n_2397547.html

The following information is from a report from the Crimes against children research center which talks about the Unknown Exaggerated Statistics of Juvenile Prostitution. Crimes against Children Research Center at the University of New Hampshire
http://humantraffickingintheusa.weebly.com

Undocumented Immigrants: Facts and Figures
http://www.urban.org/publications/1000587.html

The Hajj

(The letter that Malcolm X wrote to Alex Haley from Mecca)

The Hajj, this song was written based on a letter that Malcolm X wrote to Alex Haley while on Hajj. After receiving this letter from Khalid El-hakim from the Black History 101 Mobile Museum. As I pondered its contents and wondered if this could be made a song. I toiled over the fact that I was about to take a part of Black history and fuse it with modern culture i.e. hip-hop. As we, Public Enemy have often done infusing noteworthy historical people places and events into a body of work which gave us the ability to have our listeners think beyond our view in a song that can be limited.

It is my deepest desire to educate the next generation as to who Marcus Garvey was and his organization the UNIA and his relationship to Malcolm's parents thus affecting Malcolm X.

My intent is to show Malcolm's progression from street hustler and pimp to one of the greatest men in history not only black history but history.

There are many facets and phases that we can explore about the life of Malcolm X in this song. I wanted to focus in on what Malcolm X said his self in the letter to Alex Haley. If you read the autobiography of Malcolm X you will discover a man who was dedicated to the rise of his people. This letter is an extension of that same spirit that Malcolm X conveyed to Alex Haley. Through the medium of hip hop we have discovered a way to entertain and teach these valuable lessons while learning the depth of most of them ourselves. I hope this view of a man in history is studied remixed and understood in the best light possible.

The Hajj
Written by: K. Shah pka Professor Griff

Malcolm born a hustler but Garvey at the root
Legal guardians active life lost at the end of a noose
Young gifted and black Done but easier said,
The streets referred to him, aka Detroit red

Robbed, pimped and sold smack
In case you are wondering, hard white modern day crack
Prison bound, one of the 30 to 60 million lost n found
His brother put him up on game
From that point on nothing would be the same

He put down the drugs, the pimp and the knife
Picked up a book a pen, and Islam saved his life
Met a man, developed a bond, who put in his heart
The holy book, and the Quran in case you forgot

Face the east, walked upright live in peace
Broke camp one summer and headed east,
Muslim man, no longer, Uptown soap box prophet
Mastered 120 and knew how to drop it.

Mecca the holiest city in Islam
Non believers can't tread
Nor rest there eyes upon
From hajj to heaven
Gates from ground zero to seven
Not saying this to brag or boast

Acapella Revolution

Nor raise a glass to toast

Malcolm's open mind, treated his wife divine
The American negrow, brotherhood from white Muslims
he didn't know
Now in Jeddah, better get prayed up.
Kkkrackers named Muhammad shit didn't add up

Eaten from the same plate, drank from the same glass
Thinking this can't be real, with whites, were not in the
same class
Slept on the same rug while praying to the same god
Had to write someone about this isssshhh its very odd.

With Muslims who skin was as the whitest of white
Whose eyes were as the bluest of blue
We were all the same brothers
Because our belief in Allah was proof

As long as there Islam remained true,
Allah had wiped the white from their minds
Their behavior and their attitudes too

If white Americans would accept Islam
There would be no hatred in the west
But their racist flag and cross
Leads her in to this suicidal path of death

I'm leaving now for Egypt and the Sudan
Yea I see them, demons with no hoods like the clan

Kenya Nigeria and Ghana, meet me at the port
Then New York I'm headed uptown
Still not eating pork

Alex you gotta write fast, CIA dead on my ass
Chickens coming home to roost never made me sad
My life n death will be a mystery
Without my wife's high moral
I cannot take my place in history

I have come to realize, I have no control over their evil
plans
The gov't sent, agents from DC to Mecca and the Sudan
The death of a black leader, the devil planned It
But Allah is the best planner, From Harlem to hamtramic

Islam the only spiritual force, that can ward off
The disaster that racism must inevitably bleed off
Then at the Audubon Ballroom the crowd was out
The FBI was definitely, in the house no doubt

Commotion in the audience
Get your hand out my pocket, someone said
Shots Rang out, Malcolm X fell back and lay dead.

"I don't even call it violence when it's in self defense; I call
it intelligence."
                    ----Malcolm X

Legal guardians active life lost at the end of a noose
Young gifted and black Done but easier said,
The streets referred to him, aka Detroit red

Malcolm X was born Malcolm Little on May 19, 1925, in
Omaha, Nebraska, one of eight children. His father, Earl
Little, was a Baptist preacher who supported Marcus
Garvey's Back to Africa movement. When Malcolm was
four, the family moved to Lansing, Michigan, where Earl
tried opening a store while continuing his preaching. But a
group of white supremacists calling themselves the Black
Legion (a sub-branch of the Ku Klux Klan) became irate
to him.

Robbed, pimped and sold smack
In case you are wondering, hard white modern day crack
Prison bound, one of the 30 to 60 million lost n found
His brother put him up on game
From that point on nothing would be the same

Two years later, Earl Little was found dead on the trolley
tracks in town after a streetcar ran over him. Despite the
police report that Earl's death was an accident, Malcolm
strongly believed that his father was killed by the Black
Legion who placed his father's body on the tracks to make
it look like an accident. Following Earl's death, Malcolm's
mother, Louise Little, tried to support her eight children on
her own. Malcolm started stealing food and candy from
neighborhood stores to support his brothers and sisters.
After being caught a few too many times, a local court
ruled that Louise was unable to control Malcolm and had
him removed from her care and placed in a friendly white
couple's home who knew Louise. Two years later, Louise,

due to severe stress in raising her children, suffered a
nervous breakdown and was committed to the state mental
hospital where she remained for the remaining 26 years of
her life.

He put down the drugs, the pimp and the knife
Picked up a book a pen, and Islam saved his life
Met a man, developed a bond, who put in his heart
The holy book, and the Quran in case you forgot

After finishing 8th grade, Malcolm dropped out of school
and traveled to Boston where his older sister, Ella, lived.
After a few years, Malcolm moved to New York City to
support himself, he became a numbers runner, a drug
dealer, even a pimp. He wore zoot suits and dyed his hair
red, which earned him the nickname 'Detroit Red.' He
relocated to Boston again where he organized a robbery
ring that was uncovered by the police in 1946, and he was
sentenced to eight to ten years in prison. Malcolm used the
time behind bars to educate himself in the prison library
where he learned the fundamentals of grammar and
increased his vocabulary. It was here that a few inmates
introduced Malcolm to a new religion and movement, The
Nation of Islam. Malcolm's younger brother, Reginald,
already a member, visited him and told him about Islam
and about Allah. Much of what Reginald said confused
Malcolm, but two phrases took root in his head, "The white
man is the devil" and "The black man is the brainwashed."
Malcolm learned that if he wanted to join, he would have
to accept its theology and submit completely to its founder
and leader, Elijah Muhammad.

Face the east, walked upright live in peace
Broke camp one summer and headed east,

Muslim man, no longer, Uptown soap box prophet
Mastered 120 and knew how to drop it.

Inspired by the new direction his life was taking, Malcolm wrote Elijah Muhammad a heartfelt letter about himself and why he wanted to join. Elijah wrote back welcoming Malcolm to the faith. He instructed Malcolm to drop his last name, which his ancestors inherited from a slave owner and replace it with the letter X which symbolized that his true African name had been lost. In 1952, Malcolm was finally paroled from prison. Rather than returning to the life of crime, Malcolm committed himself to learning more about his new religion. In 1958, Malcolm married Betty Shabazz, a Muslim nurse and together they had four daughters (plus two more born after his death). Over the next several years, Malcolm became the spokesperson for the Nation of Islam and became one of its most powerful speakers attracting thousands of African-Americans into the fold with his charismatic speeches and rich and powerful words. Malcolm's charismatic personality also attracted the attention of the white media. But unlike Dr. Martin Luther King, Jr. who believed in non-violent tactics to archive equal rights for blacks, Malcolm favored the use of arms and proposed a revolutionary program that would create a separate society for blacks in America. Malcolm's relationship with the media displeased Elijah Muhammad for he felt that the Nation of Islam's messages where being overshadowed by Malcolm's newfound celebrity.

Mecca the holiest city in Islam

Non believers can't tread

Nor rest their eyes upon

From hajj to heaven

Gates from ground zero to seven

Not saying this to brag or boast

Nor raise a glass to toast

In the early 1960s, Malcolm learned of paternity suits filed by two women of the Nation of Islam who worked for Elijah Muhammad as his secretaries. Determined to get to the bottom of the rumors about Elijah Muhammad, Malcolm met with the two women and later privately with Elijah Muhammad who did not deny the accusations against him as he did publicly but justified his actions by comparing his with other Biblical figures as David and Noah who suffered from "moral lapses". Elijah's response left Malcolm dissatisfied and contributed to his growing disenchantment with the Nation of Islam.

Malcolm's open mind, treated his wife divine
The American Negro, brotherhood from white Muslims he didn't know
Now in Jeddah, better get prayed up.
Kkkrackers named Muhammad shit didn't add up

In November 1963, Malcolm's candidness with reporters provided Elijah Muhammad with an excuse to sideline him. When asked about the assassination of President John F. Kennedy, Malcolm called the murder a case of "the chickens coming home to roost." The public, both black and white, was outraged by Malcolm's comment after which Elijah suspended him from his duties as spokesperson for 90 days.

Eaten from the same plate, drank from the same glass
Thinking this can't be real, with whites, were not in the same class
Slept on the same rug while praying to the same god

Had to write someone about this isssshhh its very odd.

Feeling betrayed by the Nation of Islam, Malcolm announced in March 1964 that he was not going to return, but he was going to form his own movement called the Muslim Mosque, Inc. and invited blacks everywhere to join his new crusade. In response to Malcolm's announcement, Elijah Muhammad wrote in the Nation of Islam's bi-weekly newspaper that "only those who wish to be led to hell or to their doom will follow Malcolm. No one ever leaves the Nation of Islam."

With Muslims who skin was as the whitest of white
Whose eyes were as the bluest of blue
We were all the same brothers
Because our belief in Allah was proof

As long as there Islam remained true,
Allah had wiped the white from their minds
Their behavior and their attitudes too

If white Americans would accept Islam
There would be no hatred in the west
But their racist flag and cross
Leads her in to this suicidal path of death

I'm leaving now for Egypt and the Sudan
Yea I see them, demons with no hoods like the clan
Kenya Nigeria and Ghana, meet me at the port
Then New York I'm headed uptown
Still not eating pork

Over the next several months, several attempts were made against Malcolm's life. Apparently, this did not surprise him for he said, "This thing with me will only be resolved by death and violence." In April 1964, Malcolm made a pilgrimage to Mecca, the Islamic holy city in Saudi Arabia. The trip had a profound affect on him when he was greeted warmly by Muslims of many nationalities. Malcolm then realized that if Muslims of all races can live together in peace, why not people of all religions? Malcolm then remarked, "My true brotherhood includes people of all races, coming together as one. It has proved to me that there is the power of one God."

Alex you gotta write fast, CIA dead on my ass
Chickens coming home to roost never made me sad
My life n death will be a mystery
Without my wife's high moral
I cannot take my place in history

Upon his return to the USA, death threats continued leading to his house in Queens, New York, being fire-bombed in February 1965, to his assassination a week later at the Audubon Ballroom in Harlem, New York City, where he held weekly meetings. Although the Nation of Islam was suspected of being behind Malcolm's murder, his three killers, who were convicted of the murder, denied being part of the Nation of Islam or knowing each other despite the fact that they were Black Muslims and later revealed to be members. When questioned about Malcolm X's murder, Elijah Muhammad maintained (as he did with a lot of other things) that neither he nor his organization had anything to do with Malcolm X's assassination.

I have come to realize, I have no control over their evil plans
The gov't sent, agents from DC to Mecca and the Sudan
The death of a black leader, the devil planned It
But Allah is the best planner, From Harlem to hamtramic

Islam the only spiritual force, that can ward off
The disaster that racism must inevitably bleed off
Then at the Audubon Ballroom the crowd was out
The FBI was definitely, in the house no doubt

Commotion in the audience
Get your hand out my pocket, someone said
Shots Rang out, Malcolm X fell back and lay dead.

Resource Information:

A letter written to Alex Haley from Malcolm X while on Hajj in the Holy City of Mecca.
Malcolm X mini bio: http://www.imdb.com/name/nm0944318/bio

"No turning back"

Written by: Kavon shah pka Professor Griff

January 6th 2013

This song is for all those fathers whose children are being abused by a bitch and a bitch ass nigga whom she lives with. This is for victims of child abuse. This is to those fathers who really want to be fathers but the system of racism white supremacy is hard at work to continue to destroy the black family. This is a real situation that I am living present day.

You send threats to the vet, but you target my youngest seed

Not set tripping, but we gon see what color you really bleed

Claim I got a curse seed, claim u got crew, please!

Claim I'm a sukkah mc, click click stop pleading please get up off yo knees

Speak your piece, before my crew catches wind of this

Not trying to catch a charge so I'll encrypt the next 3 verses

Call me acting all nonchalant, with a soft tone,

Pump the breaks dude and watch your mutha fuckin tone

Gettin yo weight up in front of yo trick

Caught her on her knees, now you wanna switch the shit

Drugs and drunken fits of rage so you beat the kid

So to mask the liks my child cry's out.....she's hurt

Then you turn around an spend yo last on

Some fake boob job, And a bootleg ass purse

Naps and dirt, your a product of your environment

Put in work, doubt it, yo! next party's a retirement

First time you Broke the code and I gave yo ass a pass
This time, last time, a check that, yo stupid ass can't cash
No, I'm not bluffing I do this cuz I'm was call to it
That's my life, that's my love, Isa Shah that's my blood

This shit about to get extremely wild
You see, you never fuck with another man's child
I'm taking it personal; Maybe you feel some kinda way
UN registered pedophile, but we all knew your ass was gay anyway
You suburban boy toy seeking some hood shit
Look no further, I'm about to bring some rude boy shit
This parts the saddest, I know its a classic case of a tragic addict
Using my child's head for target practice
She told me of the temper tantrum
So Don't act tough, when I toe tag your fragments
I'm coming for it, but you ain't my main target
It's the dizzy dumb bitch, so, I beg your pardon
Got the nerve to brag about heat clapping
The ratchet you packing, In the trap Stackin
Cheddar for the rats you trapping
Now you Trying to get fly at the mouth
Red faced and angry with your little chest stuck out
In any hood I'm good, I roll on the humble
You sent 13 texts messages, with threats
Thinking I would fold n crumble
You called the "G" by his govt
Now, Immma show you just how foul it really gets
Now I see you playing all innocent

The cute roll, the victim, you know the regular bitch shit
Keep it "G" That whack pussy n pillow talk got you tripping
Flipping on the phone like you, playing me out position
Take heed to this, but remember yo! other man's and them
I put him to sleep and guess what, I'm still standing
Rethink your strategy, now, you sure you want to do this
Cuz if my daughter call me one more time
It's a rap for you and yo! Dumb bitch

Dedicated to my youngest daughter Isa Shah.

Resource Information:

This is an actual true story......I don't want to wear a t-shirt saying Isa Shah RIP

A NEW FIVE PART SERIES: DOMESTIC VIOLENCE IN THE BLACK COMMUNITY: DOMESTIC VIOLENCE AGAINST BLACK WOMEN
http://theblackfistblog.blogspot.com/2012/01/new-five-part-series-domestic-violence.html

The Statistics on Domestic Violence Are Shocking
http://www.blackwomenshealth.com/blog/domestic-violence-when-love-becomes-hurtful/

Are Black Women Invisible? Domestic Violence In The Black Community...It's Real As A Heart Attack

http://www.blackloveandmarriage.com/2011/10/are-
black-women-invisible-domestic-violence-in-the-black-
community-its-real-as-a-heart-attack/

Community Violence

A comparison of delinquent and non-delinquent youth
found that a history of family violence or abuse is the most
significant difference between the two groups (Miller, G.
"Violence By and Against America's Children," Journal of
Juvenile Justice Digest, XVII(12) p.6. 1989)

According to the United States Department of Justice, law
enforcement agencies arrested approximately 2.8 million
juveniles in 1997. Of that number, 2,500 were arrested for
murder and 121,000 for other violent crimes. Juveniles
accounted for 19% of all arrests, 14% of murder arrests,
and 17% of all violent crime arrests. (Juvenile Offenders
and Victims: 1999 National Report, Office of Juvenile
Justice and Delinquency Prevention)

In 1997, the National Center for Health Statistics listed
homicide as the fourth leading cause of death for children
ages 1 through 4, third for youth ages 5 through 14, and
second for persons ages 15 through 24. (National Center
for Health Statistics. Death Rates for Selected Causes, by
5-year Age Groups 1997.)

The U.S. has the highest rates of childhood homicide,
suicide, and firearm-related death among industrialized
countries. (CDC's Morbidity and Mortality Weekly
Report, February 7, 1997, Vol 46, No. 5, Rates of
Homicide, Suicide, and Firearm-Related Death Among
Children ñ 26 Industrialized Countries.)

http://www.nccev.org/violence/statistics/statistics-community.html

Protecting Against Child Predators: Beyond Stranger Danger
How to give your child the facts he'll need to protect himself
http://childparenting.about.com/od/healthsafety/a/Protecting-Against-Child-Predators-Beyond-Stranger-Danger.htm

How to Defend Against Parental Alienation Allegations
http://www.custodyprepformoms.org/pas.htm

List of Websites

http://www.blackhistory101mobilemuseum.com

http://www.youtube.com/professorgriff

http://www.publicenemy.com

http://www.hdqtrz.com

http://www.youtube.com/nmemindz

https://twitter.com/realprofgriff

http://blackconsciousness.com (for books and dvd's)

Take the black IQ test at http://blackconsciousness.com/

http://www.finalcall.com

http://www.blackelectorate.com

http://www.daveyd.com

http://whatreallyhappened.com

http://jordanmaxwell.com

http://www.infowars.com

http://rense.com

http://www.educate-yourself.org

http://www.ancient-knowledge-breakthrough.net/index.html

http://www.gemworld.com/USAvsUS.htm

http://astro.temple.edu/~rgreene/BlackComp/

http://www.dickgregory.com/

http://www.suzar.com/

http://www.blackgenocide.org/home.html

http://www.drsebiproducts.com/

http://www.DAGHETTOTYMZ.COM/main.html

http://www.blacknews.com/

List of African Centered Books

Books by Dr. Ben

Books by Ivan Van Sertima

Books by Dr. John Henrik Clarke

Books by Minister Louis Farrakhan

To the Black Man in America by Elijah Muhammad

Stolen Legacy by George GM James

The Destruction of Black Civilization by Chancellor Williams

The Isis Papers by Dr. Frances Cress Welsing

Black Out Through White Wash by Suzar

Two Thousand Seasons by Ayi Kwei Armah

How Europe Underdeveloped Africa by W. Rodney

The Falsification of African Consciousness by Amos Wilson

Awakening the Natural Genius of Black Children by Amos Wilson

Echoes of the Old Darkland by Charles S. Finch

The Science of Melanin: Dispelling the Myths by T. Owens Moore

African Holistic Health by Laila Africa

Nutricide: The Nutritional Destruction of the Black Race by Laila Africa

The Miseducation of the Black Child by Nathan Hare

Let the circle be unbroken by African spirituality in the Diaspora by M. Ani

Survival Strategies for Africans in America by Anthony Browder

100 Amazing Facts about the Negro by J.A. Rogers

The Egyptian Philosophers by Molefi Kete Asante

African Presence in Early Asia by Charles Finch

Civilization and Barbarism by C.A. Diop

African Origin of Civilization by Cheikh Anta Diop

The Cultural Unity of Black Africa by C. A. Diop

Black Africa: The Economic and Cultural Basis by Cheikh Anta Diop

Decolonising the Afrikan Mind by Dr. Alim Bey

Black African Hair and The Insanity of the Black Blonde Psych by Rych McCain

The Goddess Blackwoman by Akil

ASAFO: A Warrior's Guide to Manhood by Mwalimu K. Bomani Baruti

The Mystical and Magical Paths of Self and Not-self by Paul Simons

The Sex Imperative by Mwalimu K. Bomani Baruti

Brainwashed by Tom Burrell

Opening To Spirit by Caroline Shola Arewa

Awakening the Master Feminine by Yao Niamey Morris

Auras and Chakras by Fiona Toy

Energy Healing for Beginners by Ruth White

The True Authorship of the New Testament by Abelard Reuchlin

List of NWO/Illuminati books

Books:

1. Codex Magica Secret Signs, Mysterious Symbols, and Hidden Codes of the Illuminati

2. Mysterious Monuments: Encyclopedia of Secret Illuminati

3. Mysterious Monuments-Encyclopedia of Secret Illuminati Designs Mason-Texe Marrs

4. Kymatica Dvd Esoteric Agenda 2 Illuminati NWO 2012

5. Top 13 Illuminati Bloodlines and Their Mind Control 2 Dvd Set New World Order

6. Exposing The Illuminati From Within: New Age & Satanism David Icke Black Magic of Power Dvd Illuminati 9/11 Conspiracy New World Order NWO 2012 Empire

List of NWO/Illuminati dvd's

DVD'S

Ring of Power Dvd Illuminati 9/11 Conspiracy
New World Order NWO 2012 Empire

Occult world of commerce
DVD/JordanMaxwell/Illuminati

Behold a Pale Horse DVD William Bill Cooper
UFO NWO Illuminati 2012 David Icke

The Arrivals DVD Dajjal Anti-Christ Religion
Illuminati NWO Wake Up Project 2012

Kymatica Esoteric Agenda DVD Set Illuminati
2012 New Age NWO 2012 Evolution

HAARP Project Dvd Tesla Conspiracy Illuminati
2012 Weather Modification NWO

George Orwell 1984 Dvd New World Order NWO
Illuminati Rfid Classic Sci Fi

Cia Mind Control Dvd Trance Formation
Conspiracy Nwo Illuminati 2012 hypnosis

Loose Change 4th Edition An American Coup
DVD 99 Mins NWO Illuminati Conspiracy

List of Books and DVD'S for your Live –it vs your DIE-it

1.   **Medisin: The Causes & Solutions to Disease, Malnutrition, And the Medical Sins that Are Killing the World** by: Scott Whitaker

2.   **Nutricide: The Nutritional Destruction of the Black Race** by Dr Llaila O. Africa

3.   **African Holistic Health** by Dr Llaila O. Afrika

4.   **Dictionary of Vitamins and Minerals from A to Z** by Llaila O. Afrika

5.   **Handbook for Raising Black Children** by Llaila Afrika

6.   **Drugs Masquerding As Foods "Killing American-Afrikans & All Peoples"** by Suzar, N.D., D.M.

7.   **African Origin of Biological Psychiatry** by Richard King

8.   **Melanin: A key to Freedom** by Richard King

9.   **African Psychology: Toward its Reclamation, Reascension and Revitalization** by W. Nobles

10.   **Fat Sick And Nearly Dead** by A Joe cross film http://www.fatsickandnearlydead.com/Licensed to kill

11.   **Super charge your immune system** by: Gary Null

http://www.maketheconsciousconnection.com/tag/center-your-health/Diet for a free America

The Psychological Covert War on Hip Hop --- $25.00
Analytixz --- $20.00
Accapella Revolution --- $20.00

To place an order online through PayPal:
PCW --- PCWHipHop@gmail.com
Analytixz --- 7thoctave@gmail.com
Acapella Revolution --- 7thoctave@gmail.com
(In the "message box" please indicate which book you want to
Order
)

QTY	DESCRIPTION	UNIT PRICE	TOTAL

PAYABLE TO HEIRZ TO THE SHAH:
MAIL PAYMENTS TO:

KAVON SHAH
P.O. BOX 11902
ATLANTA, GA 30355

SUBTOTAL	
SHIPPING AND HANDLING	$4.95
TOTAL	

Acapella Revolution

Please print clearly, so we may get the book to the correct address

Name:_____

Address:_____

City:_____

State:_____

Zip:_____

Telephone:_____

Please allow 2 weeks for Domestic shipping and 3 weeks for International shipping.

4/29/16

CPSIA information can be obtained at www.ICGtesting.com
Printed in the USA
LVOW07s1452120116

470291LV00015B/990/P